General Editors' Preface

The books in this series provide information and advice on a wide range of educational issues for teachers who are busy, yet who are concerned to keep abreast of new developments.

The aim is practicality: slim volumes that are sources of authoritative help and swift reference, written and edited by people whose expertise in their field is backed up by experience of the everyday realities of school and classroom. The books are planned to cover well-defined topics relevant to schools in widely differing situations: subject teaching, curriculum development, areas of responsibility within schools, and the relationship of the school to the community. They are published at a time when there is a growing call for increased professional accountability in our primary and secondary schools. The 'in-service between covers' that characterizes these handbooks is designed to contribute to the vitality and development of schools and of the individuals within them.

The author of this book has long and varied experience as a teacher of drama. She holds that the subject of drama is human relationships. Through its imaginative pursuit pupils can be brought to question the clichés of thought that inhibit their understanding of themselves and of others so that on occasions they can come 'to glimpse universal truths beyond their actions'. As well as making a strong case for drama for its own sake she shows its value as a device for exploring aspects of a variety of other school subjects.

The book has a realistic and positive tone. Readers with little or no experience of conducting drama in the classroom have the benefit of very specific advice. Her guidance on how to control the development of a lesson should reassure those who fear matters might get out of hand. There are many references to actual lessons, to moments of difficulty surmounted as well as to instances of evident easy success, with helpfully frequent quotation of the words used by both teacher and pupils at such classroom turning points. The coherent and personal approach of the author makes the book as valuable to the teacher experienced in drama as to the newcomer conducting a lesson for the first time.

Teaching

General Editors: Sydney Hill and Colin Reid

Approaching Classroom Drama

Rosemary Linnell

Advisory Teacher in Drama, ILEA

Edward Arnold

A division of Hodder & Stoughton

LONDON   MELBOURNE   AUCKLAND

© 1982 Rosemary Linnell

First publication in Great Britain 1982
Fourth impression 1989

British Library Cataloguing in Publication Data
  Linnell, Rosemary
  Approaching classroom drama — (Teaching matters)
  1. Drama — Study and teaching
  I. Title   II. Series
  792'.071   PN1701
ISBN 0 7131 0724 3

Printed and bound in Great Britain for Edward Arnold, the
educational, academic and medical publishing division of Hodder and
Stoughton Limited, Mill Road, Dunton Green, Sevenoaks, Kent,
by Athenaeum Press Ltd, Newcastle upon Tyne.

Contents

Introduction	vii
1 The aims and uses of classroom drama	1
The nature of dramatic activity	1
Acting—the suspension of disbelief	2
Performance—communication to others	5
2 The role of the teacher	8
The classic model	8
The function of a drama teacher	10
Definitions of drama	12
The teacher as an observer	13
3 Introducing drama	17
The drama room, organizing space	17
The lesson plan	18
Control factors and teaching techniques	20
Beginning the lesson	25
4 Strategies	33
Teaching in role	33
Acquiring necessary skills	36
5 Developing and deepening the drama	42
Building belief	42
Subject matter	45
Planning a sequence of lessons	47
Developing language	50
6 Lessons	58
7 Theatre as an art form	76
Performance	76
Theatre Arts for examination	77
Performance as an art	79
Conclusion	82
Appendix: Resources	84
Bibliography	87

Introduction

A chance group of about forty teachers, from both primary and secondary schools, were asked whether they thought drama should feature in every child's education. They all agreed that it should and offered the following reasons: to increase confidence, to enable the individual to work as part of a group, to encourage a growth in language ability, to promote self-expression in words and movement, to put oneself in another person's shoes, to develop the imagination, to increase the ability to memorize and make sense of dramatic literature, to reinforce learning by enacting stories and situations, to handle difficult concepts and emotions in controlled surroundings, to enjoy a communal activity, to learn to see the funny side of things, to motivate other forms of learning, to develop sensitivity, to learn to relax, to develop a critical faculty, to learn to concentrate.

Having compiled such a formidable list of reasons for doing drama, these same teachers were asked how many of them actually taught drama in their own schools. Only four replied in the affirmative.

Maybe they were shy or reluctant to admit it, but most of them said that they were afraid to try, that they might lose control, that other teachers complained of the noise, that use of the hall was restricted, that, most of all, they did not know how to begin, that they were likely to lose face with their classes and that their failure as teachers would be more public than it would be with other subjects on the curriculum. Some admitted that they had tried and produced only chaos, others said that they had been put off by their own experience as students when taking part in badly run drama lessons which had left them feeling exposed and insecure; others had seen examples of such professional work in fully-fledged performances of school plays that they felt inadequate in trying to compete on the same level. One said that in his opinion, drama was the most challenging and difficult activity any teacher could undertake and he was waiting until he felt more sure of his ability to teach at all, before he tested himself over that particular hurdle.

This book is dedicated to those teachers and others like them, whatever their subject or experience and whatever the age of the children they teach, who would like to include drama as part of their work with young people, but feel reluctant to take the plunge. It acknowledges that drama is a difficult and challenging subject, which nevertheless can have enormous rewards and achievements, as evinced by the objectives included in that long list of 'reasons for doing drama'. Not all those objectives are considered in this book. Memorizing dramatic literature, for example, is rather a specific skill, and re-enacting a well-known story is probably not the most effective way of learning. The purpose of this book is to examine the nature of dramatic activity so that teachers may be able to decide, moment by moment, what it is their pupils are looking for, and having perceived the need, may be able to supply the appropriate dramatic structure to satisfy that need and to lead on to further understanding.

Rather than prescribe any single method of teaching drama, this book examines the various kinds of drama available to young people and the function of different styles of dramatic activity, so that the teacher can begin from the standpoint of the childrens' own work and, using that as a basis, extend the work of the class beyond their normal boundaries. It will examine some aims and objectives for drama lessons, the strategies that may be usefully employed to obtain those objectives, and some ways of evaluating the work done in drama lessons in order to plan ahead more successfully for the future. There is no strict division into Infant, Junior or Secondary classroom practice; examples are drawn from lessons involving children of all ages. The emphasis is strongly on classroom drama, leaving aside the production of the school play which, to do it justice, would require more space than is available in this short handbook.

No book can make drama teaching easy. There is nothing to be gained from a collection of simple drama games and movement exercises. As any student teacher will know, the only outcome of that ploy is to go on providing more and yet more parlour games until the children are bored and the ideas run dry. The best drama teaching uses only those methods and skills that are part of the equipment of any teacher: a sympathetic understanding of how children think and feel, a wide range of vocal skills, imagination, and above all curiosity. The most exciting drama happens most often with the greatest economy of ideas. All a book can do is to offer teachers a few pointers to making drama accessible to themselves and to their pupils.

1
The aims and uses of classroom drama

The nature of dramatic activity

Some kind of dramatic activity forms part of the cultural pattern of most human communities. Dramatic play is also part of the growth and development of all young humans. Therefore the teacher who includes an element of dramatic activity in her lessons, is extending and drawing upon the natural elements of human behaviour in the same way as the earliest Greek dramatists.

Audiences in a theatre of any kind are engaged in reflecting upon human behaviour: observing the actions of their fellow beings in a social context. Actors, dancers and dramatists pick out certain elements of behaviour, simplify them and present them in such a way that we are able to recognize those same traits in ourselves and thereby identify with the figures on stage. This may be either reassuring or quite disturbing. It may make profound sense of something previously unrecognized, it may confirm an attitude, or even make it seem ridiculous. The place of theatre in any society is usually closely allied to that society's beliefs, and the same need that exists in a growing civilization, to play out legends and rituals, exists in the growing child who acts out his own 'legends'.

There is a true story which illustrates this very clearly. A small child was afraid of the dark. However, she could not define 'the dark' in her own mind, so invented a 'Big Bad Wolf' who lived on the dark landing outside her bedroom door. Her mother began to explain away this fear by saying that wolves could not live in a semi-detached house with people and dogs around, but then, realizing the purpose this imaginary wolf was serving, she went along with the child's pretence, asking questions about the nature of the wolf, whether it lived alone and where it slept and so on. The child invented circumstances that explained her fear in rational terms that were acceptable to her and also, by implication, less frightening than the large, generalized fear of the dark. The wolf gradually, over several months, whenever she remembered it, acquired a mate, several cubs, lived in a bookcase, and eventually moved into the lavatory, where it could be controlled by the magic spell operated by so many children: 'If you can get out of the room before the water goes whoosh, you're quite safe.' This mythical story served the child in the same way as a communal myth serves civilization. By allowing her to develop her own story, the child's mother gave her a satisfactory way of explaining and accepting her own fears and emotions. The mother did not develop or change the story, but went along with the belief and was an audience for the pretence.

Often children themselves act out such 'legends' using caricature and grotesque 'Punch-like' crudities such as that of the demented, screaming teacher, impotently thwacking at his pupils, or that of the unbelievably ill-mannered family at breakfast. Everyone knows that these are crude symbols, that such things are not totally realistic, but that they contain enough truth to have been recognized by generation after generation of young children over the last hundred years. This is 'playground' drama and there are not many teachers who would want it to feature largely in their classrooms, just as there are not many children who would wish their teachers to participate in these plays. They are, however, an important part of dramatic activity and a perceptive teacher will recognize the elements of such ritual caricature and will know when it is appropriate to the class.

In classroom drama children are not often the audience, although they may learn a good deal from watching and observing from the sidelines. More often than not the child in the classroom is in the unique position of being the actor, the dramatist and the audience more or less at the same time and it is this richness of experience that makes drama such a useful way of learning about the complexities of human behaviour.

The function of the drama teacher is to find a way of enabling this learning to happen. To do this successfully it is necessary to understand what is so special about dramatic activity.

In the first place, it is important to recognize that drama makes emotional demands as well as physical and intellectual ones. It is often difficult to think of education as concerning itself with emotion. That may be one reason why teachers find the whole concept of teaching drama rather daunting. There is, however, one very important factor to take into consideration: *Drama takes place as part of a fictional or imagined situation and therefore it is different from real life.*

Because it is not real (and this is not at all the same as saying it is not realistic), it can stop at any moment. Once it has stopped, the participants in the drama can allow themselves to reflect upon human behaviour, their own and other people's. By abstracting certain responses and qualities and by being able to examine and even to replay some of them, we are using the special quality of theatrical form as a method of education.

Acting—the suspension of disbelief

To examine the nature of this fictional element in drama let us look first at the nature of acting, because this is what we want our pupils to do, even though we do not want them to become actors in any professional sense. In the dictionary sense of the word, to act is to do, to undertake *an action*, but in our sense of the word, acting is the exercise of belief in a totally fictional situation. There are usually two important elements in a professional actor's job. One happens early on when he is struggling to establish the reality of his belief in what Constantin Stanislavsky called the 'Big Lie'; the other happens when the actor selects from that experience the qualities of that belief which will communicate themselves to other people. In the professional theatre the first usually happens in rehearsal, often in total privacy. The second is what is needed to create an effective performance.

No performer can afford to believe with total intensity in everything the character does, so he selects the appropriate symbols. Such symbols may take the form of a significant gesture, a tone of voice, or the use of some object such as a cigarette holder or a crown. A whole sequence of movement, mime or poetry may provide a satisfactory symbolic expression of a mood or situation. Sometimes a symbol can arouse even clearer responses than an attempt at recreating total belief. The teacher using drama needs to be able to distinguish between the two, so that wherever necessary she can either aim for the most appropriate use of symbolism or discard it and go for total belief because nothing else will do.

Very young children and actors share the same ability—to be able to pick up and put down pretence at will. It is this facility, to go into a pretend situation with absolute sincerity and belief, that is at the core of all drama activity and yet it is this that is so often the greatest stumbling block of all. Without the willing suspension of disbelief no real theatre can happen. An audience in a theatre has gone there specifically to achieve that very thing: they want to suspend their disbelief, they want to be 'taken out of themselves'.

The child in a classroom needs the same suspension of disbelief before the fictional situation can assume any kind of reality, before it can function as drama. Yet he is not in a theatre, he has not been offered the same aids to transport him into a make-believe world. There is no darkened anonymity, no curtain to move aside to reveal another, more exciting place. He has to do what the actor does in rehearsal, create out of his own feelings something that seems real and is believable. Not only that: he is also sharing the moment with other children who are in the room with him but who are not necessarily at the same stage of 'pretending' as he is.

To set up anything like a successful drama lesson in academic surroundings depends entirely upon the teacher's ability to create and sustain belief in the minds of her pupils. Like the actor, the class first have to believe in the fictional situation. Like the audience they can be helped to suspend disbelief by being offered an appropriate set of symbolic actions with which they can identify and to which they may respond.

If young children can so easily enter into the world of make-believe, why is it that as they grow older they can become so inhibited?

There are many answers to this question and the drama teacher needs to be aware of all of them, if she is going to ask a class to suspend disbelief.

In the first place, the young child's ability to pretend is a very necessary way of trying out behaviour before arriving at the appropriate situation. In playing school, mothers and fathers, doctors and nurses and so on, the child enacts his own appreciation of future roles. Later on the child perceives more about the reality of the world around him and makes less obvious use of imaginative play. This does not mean that pretence ceases, but it often becomes more personal and secret. At this stage, at least in public, he will use a more socially acceptable form of imaginative play such as setting up a gang house, or playing soldiers.

Second, the degree of belief in an 'as if' or 'pretend' situation can be quite startling to the person taking part. If there is some blurring between what is real and what is not real, then children can be confused and even frightened by their own belief. The older the child is and the more aware he is of his own development as a person, the more he needs to be reassured about the *impermanence of unreality*. It is very important for him to keep a secure hold on the real world whilst at the same time using his imagination to the full.

Third, it may well be that a child will be told to grow up, to stop being silly or not to tell lies when he is pretending or testing out the power of pretence on other people. So again it is important that in establishing a dramatic pretence both pupil and teacher know exactly what is happening and agree on a mutual suspension of disbelief.

This all assumes that imaginative drama work is a goal to be desired, which may sound like a truism; however, it happens far too often that drama lessons are concerned with acting techniques and that little or no real belief is ever called for. Far too often teachers set their classes vigorous physical exercises and give them suggestions like 'imagine you are an old man'. It is not easy for any child to have to look round a room of seemingly arthritic manikins assuming the posture of old men, and believe in the reality of the pretence. It is more likely that he will remain very aware of himself and his fellows and the absurdity of the whole process will be borne in on him. Because some children can successfully imitate the behaviour of other people, they are said to be 'acting', but without believing in it themselves it remains mere imitation. They have already proceeded to the second stage, that of selecting gesture and symbolic action, while at the same time there are others in the room who are struggling towards creating a believable situation, and still others who are behaving like an audience, looking about and remaining on the fringes of the activity. To avoid such confusion it is very necessary to be quite clear about what it is we want to achieve with any class, and then to find a way to build the necessary belief. This is the key to success in any work which exercises the imagination and it is essential to all class-room drama.

It is very important that a distinction should be made between the kind of drama that provides an immediate experience, almost a surprise, for those taking part, and the drama that exists for the purpose of communicating something to other people. If we recognize the drama of surprise or immediate experience as the same as the 'Big Lie' or 'pretend-ing', we can give that a name and call that 'acting'. We can also recognize the second stage reached by all those working in the professional theatre and by some, but not all, children: the need to communicate, using voice, body and expression, those ideas that are important to them. We can give that a name, too. We can call that 'performance'. These rather arbitrary distinctions are necessary in order to be absolutely clear in our own minds what our aims or objectives are for every piece of drama-work we do with our classes. Acting and performance can happen in the same lesson with class and teacher moving from one to another almost imper-ceptibly. Both are important and often a child who is acting with a deep belief and intensity can, at the same time, be communicating with sym-bolic actions to others in the same situation. Conversely the repetition of well recognized, symbolic actions can lead to deeply felt belief. Never-theless, by knowing exactly what is implied by either mode, the teacher can encourage the use of a variety of techniques whenever they may seem appropriate.

Performance—communication to others

Many adults looking back on their schooldays remember the time when they appeared in the school play. It created an indelible effect which remains when many other important moments have been forgotten.

In our definition of performance there seems little to explain why there should be so much potency in this experience that many people carry a remembrance of it into adult life. If it is such a memorable factor of one's schooldays is it therefore a desirable part of education?

In the first place, there is obviously a major difference between the performance element in classroom drama and large-scale public perform-ance. It is almost certainly public performance that most people remem-ber so vividly and it is probably because they were acutely nervous at the time that the occasion sticks in their mind. There was almost certainly a feeling of exceptional apprehension and a heightened tension, with a rush of adrenalin which made the individual feel 'high' or somehow exhilar-ated. Certainly one behaves in a way that is unlike one's normal self. To some this can be exciting and pleasurable, to others it can be acutely unpleasant. Some people surpass themselves, others are overcome and acquit themselves badly. If the performer overcomes the fear and copes with the increased tension he may gain a supreme sense of power, which will probably be reinforced by the response of the audience and the nature of the performance as a group activity. No wonder that this sense of power has been recognized as a religious experience in so many parts of the world.

The actor in performance has awakened a response in a large number of people. By his words and actions he has made hundreds of people laugh, cry, or be afraid. Their response has been emotional rather than logical or rational. It has involved large, primitive forces which we all share but which we cannot understand. Coupled with this sense of having the power to arouse feelings in others, is the performer's sense of having survived his original fear and made positive use of the extra flood of adrenalin. His body may read this purely chemical message almost as if he had taken part in some life and death struggle and survived. It may even produce the same symptoms of shock, such as breathlessness, crying, trembling, laughing or talking nonsense afterwards, in the relief of having overcome the physical fear and tension.

What the teacher has to consider is whether such a potentially powerful element of school experience should of necessity be a part of her work. Obviously if one could ensure that every child would gain the sense of power given by a successful performance, then it should be a part of everyone's experience. On the other hand because some children may react badly and suffer from stage-fright, is this a reason for excluding an element of performance from all school drama? More often than not a degree of compromise is arrived at, whereby the teacher structures her classroom work so that a certain amount of performance is included. This leaves the big, public occasion for extra-curricular work, such as that found in many drama clubs and voluntary after-school rehearsals, where those who find a pleasurable excitement in performance may extend themselves more fully.

For the most part the value of performance lies in the group creation of a piece of living art. It is this process, terminating in communication to an audience, that is important. This means that a group of people wish to select for themselves and for others a set of recognizable truths about human behaviour *because they feel they have something important to share.*

During the process of working on these important ideas they may use their own words, symbols and actions, or they may use those of a dramatist. Either way they will experiment, and include or reject a large number of ideas until they have arrived at a form which they feel best communicates itself to others. Human beings have a strong need to communicate. Even very young babies practise those actions which will awaken suitable responses in their parents. Refining and disciplining words, gestures and actions to the point where a shared response can be elicited from a group of other people is an immediate and very satisfactory art form. The fact that it is not fixed, but is ephemeral and capable of subtleties and changes, is an added bonus. The further addition of heightened circumstances of concentration and shared group sensitivity can create an exceptionally satisfying experience, providing always that the need for communication is there. What is not so beneficial is the drilled performance of a part in a play, which is being undertaken for reasons that have more to do with public relations than artistic creativity. Many teachers will have nothing to do with such activities and claim that they have little to do with classroom drama. For the most part this is true; the teacher who wishes to use drama as a means of learning is usually not concerned with performance in the same sense of the word as is the head teacher who wants to bring parents in to see the children perform a play at Christmas. There is, however, a value for some children, especially the older ones, in the study and practice of theatre as an art form. It would be a shame if there were no teachers willing and able to make this a satisfying and extending part of their education. There are also techniques which can help to make the performance of the statutory Christmas play a real experience for even the youngest performers and there are ways of ensuring that the audience responds to the symbols placed before it—ritualized images of angels, for example, and the singing of old familiar carols—whereby little is demanded of the performers, but a great deal of pleasure is given to everyone taking part in the ceremony whether performing or watching. On such occasions it is really the audience who create the emotion and it is important to recognize that it is this that forms the greatest difference between 'acting' and 'performance'.

The teacher in the classroom is very often in the position of a performer, selecting and presenting material to the class in order to elicit some response. This happens in a good deal of teaching: reading a story, for example, when the 'audience', whilst remaining quite silent, will be caught up in imagination. In a drama lesson the teacher can use a little of this skill to present imaginative situations and thoughts to the class in such a way that the chosen words and gestures may elicit an emotional response and drama can begin. Teachers are performers a good deal of the time and children are often audiences. In a drama lesson this situation can be used to stimulate drama, and the class can go on to become performers themselves to stimulate others to respond, or they can become actors in a very creative and personal field of imaginative work. There are several examples of the way in which a teacher can use her normal classroom skills to begin drama work in the section on *beginning a lesson*.

2

The role of the teacher

Some years ago there was a widely held theory in all arts teaching that a class needed only some sort of stimulus for their ideas and that they would then follow their own creative patterns, finally producing a finished piece that was all their own work. This theory led to the idea that, in the case of drama, teachers had only to produce the title for a piece of improvization, or a poem or a record to serve as a stimulus for a piece of movement or dance-drama. They could then watch the class working at their own level, offer helpful advice, and comment on the final performance, or showing, of the work.

The disadvantage of this method of working is that drama is primarily concerned with human behaviour: it is also a group activity. Many young people need help before they can work creatively as part of a group and since this ability is often seen as one of the main objectives in educational drama, the teacher needs to play an active part in encouraging helpful group dynamics. It is also by no means usual for a class to achieve greater insight into their work when left to their own devices week after week, than if the teacher is actively concerned to help in shaping their efforts.

The role of the drama teacher is to create and select learning areas which are appropriate to each class; to gain the trust of the pupils so that they may reveal their imaginings; to extend the area of their experience; to facilitate their ideas so that they achieve the utmost satisfaction from their work; to challenge the class to develop in unexpected directions; to help in the process of self-determination and self-discipline within a class and to create a responsible attitude towards the suspension of disbelief.

The classic model

To find a perfect model for the ideal drama teacher it might be useful to look at children's literature. In some classic children's books we find characters who could facilitate imaginative learning in an extraordinary fashion, although they did not behave in the usual way we expect teachers to behave. Let us take just three examples: the Psammead in E. Nesbit's *Five Children and It*, Merlin in T. H. White's *The Once and Future King* and Puck in Kipling's *Puck of Pook's Hill*.

Each began by analyzing the children's needs: not necessarily what they said they wanted, but what lay behind that stated desire—the appropriate learning area. Each then created an imaginary situation to which the children were transported. Because the children knew that this was an imaginary situation they also knew that it was finite. Because it could come to an end at any time and because it was not really happening 'here and now', it could contain elements of real risk. Death is not unthinkable. Heroism, self-sacrifice, danger and fear are all respectable parts of the situation.

The Psammead, Merlin and Puck are also themselves quite contentious characters. They can be challenging, irascible, illogical, elusive and prone to sulking. They hardly ever answer direct questions with direct answers: the children have to come up with the answers themselves.

All three, within their authors' own structures, use an elevated style of language. In their company one expects to be capable of handling complex themes and situations and confronting unusual characters with a command of appropriate style in words and behaviour.

Naturally all three characters use magic, but if we examine the way the magic worked we can see that it contains three elements that can be of significance to the teacher in the classroom. In the first place, the dramatic situation came about because all the participants agreed that it should, and were in the right frame of mind to believe in what was about to happen. Secondly, everyone was in the same play together even though they might appear in another shape or seem to be behaving untypically. Thirdly, there was usually some form of ritual which could either begin or end the imaginary adventure, so that one knew that it was going to begin when one was ready and that after it had ended the real world would take over at a given word. (Ritual is an important part of magic, of course, just as it is an important part of the drama lesson.)

One other element common to all three, which is most important to creative drama work, is that none of the participants knew beforehand what was going to happen, or if they had an inkling they kept it very much to themselves. The idea that you have to be in possession of the facts of the story beforehand, takes away all the surprise and excitement from a piece of imaginative work. Both teacher and pupils will gain tremendously from allowing the plot to develop under their noses, as it were, rather than repeating a well-known narrative. Drama does not necessarily follow any definition of narrative. Even in the theatre a play may concentrate on a mere moment in a whole saga. It is therefore the function of the teacher to decide on the experience that the class most needs, and help them to participate in it, rather than to explain away the excitement by telling the story first and asking the children to reproduce it in familiar words and movements which they feel they must 'get right'.

By accepting the relevance of these examples from literature we can ensure that our pupils achieve the same imaginative excitement and depth of learning as the children in the stories, even in the more prosaic circumstances of the classroom. Unfortunately, unlike the fictional characters it is sometimes difficult for the teacher to establish an appropriate relationship in the drama lesson. This difficulty is often caused by the image that young people have of the function of a teacher. To many children in a large number of schools, the teacher is the person who knows all the answers. However, the whole body of human behaviour, which is the subject matter of all drama, is not something one 'knows'. There may be innumerable aspects of humanity in which the children are more likely to be expert than the teacher. Therefore the teacher is there to help the class to focus their work, to set the problems or to select from those presented by the class without offering the absolute, in terms of an answer.

This can be a very disturbing attitude from the point of view of the class as they have a right to expect that a teacher will give reassuring answers to their questions. Fortunately drama itself provides the solution, because the nature of the activity demands acceptance, for the time being, of the truth that lies in the drama. For example, if the class is, in imagination, in a remote valley at dead of night with the enemy camped all round, then the problems of getting the horses out without giving the alarm are such that no classroom teacher is likely to be able to answer them. The participants themselves will have to use their own resources to solve that dilemma. If the teacher is also a participant in the same imaginary situation then her answer is of no more value than anyone else's.

This is why it is important to establish a working relationship from the start. This relationship depends on the nature of the work, and it may well be that a teacher who establishes one way of working, in let us say an English lesson, will vary the approach drastically in a drama lesson with the same class. This need not be confusing as long as the class accepts that drama requires a different set of learning procedures. It is almost as if teacher and pupils were about to conduct a number of scientific experiments together, the outcome of which could not be predicted. The teacher can help to set up the experiment but is no more likely than anyone else to be able to determine the solution.

The function of a drama teacher

Having established, in the previous section, some of the many responsibilities of a drama teacher, we should now consider how they may best be carried out. First of all it is important to realize that although successful drama teaching requires no special acting ability or actor's training, nevertheless there are certain skills which actors and drama teachers have in common.

The most important is the ability to believe in an 'as if' or pretend situation. Unless the teacher can demonstrate her ability to suspend disbelief, why should the children? It is surely not only illogical but counter-productive to suggest, even by implication, that the activity you wish the children to engage in is one that is beneath your dignity. Therefore, the first requirement of any drama teacher is the ability to share in some measure the imaginative activity of the class.

The teacher may find it useful to practise some of the techniques used in training actors. For example, looking people straight in the eye (eye contact) whilst conveying a serious belief in an imaginary situation, is often exceptionally difficult for many people; so that although specialized training in acting is not necessary, it can be useful to join a drama class oneself in order to keep in tune and to share in an imaginative exercise, as a participant, at one's own level.

Although many excellent drama teachers never take part themselves, it is nevertheless easier to learn how to teach from inside the drama, as one of the participants, than it is to learn how to influence the lesson from outside. Therefore a fair amount of this book will be spent on the techniques of teaching 'in role'. This simply supposes a willingness on the part of the teacher to share a belief in the situation. It does *not* mean that the teacher has to acquire a performer's skill in communicating a detailed or observed characterization to other people.

The drama teacher can also benefit from developing the actor's ability to 'tune in' to other people. It is important when working with a group of children to read accurately their needs, relationships and level of understanding, at any given moment. Teaching drama is never a matter of 'open your books at page four and answer the questions'. Drama teachers have to learn how to ask questions, but they rarely have any answers. The ability to listen, *and really listen*, to what children are saying (not just in the words spoken, but in the way the words are spoken) is vitally important. Equally important is the ability to read 'body language'. To be able to assess the mood of a group by the way they come into a room or sit down, is a skill shared by teachers and actors, simply because they need to develop it in order to survive. The drama teacher has to work according to the mood of the class and she must also be aware of how much her own body language and vocal colouring contribute to the mood of the class. Many teachers are unaware of how much antagonism they provoke by projecting an unconscious image of superiority, indifference, or dislike.

It is evident that classroom drama, because it deals with human behaviour, is often useful in handling and exploring difficult emotional situations amongst young people. There is, however, a temptation to look at school drama as useful therapy. Drama may be therapeutic, it often is, but the teacher who sets out to provide psycho-drama for a group needs to be very secure in her practice. It is also, unfortunately, often the case that a school will think of drama as therapy and give the opportunity for drama lessons only to the troublesome classes, often the less able children, who have difficulty adjusting to the normal disciplines of school life. This is a situation that can often be very productive, if the teacher is willing and interested in drama as therapy, but it should not be regarded as the normal place for drama in the curriculum. A teacher who is just beginning to teach the subject is well advised to recognize that there are minimum conditions which facilitate drama. Sometimes these conditions involve physical surroundings and sometimes they involve the make-up of the group. In the section on *The drama room* the minimum requirements of a teaching space are considered and the section on *Acquiring necessary skills* mentions some of the minimum social skills that a class requires before embarking on classroom drama.

The teacher functions within the lesson in a number of ways depending on the demands made on her. This means that it is difficult to say what kind of teacher a drama teacher should be. It is easier to say something about the various kinds of drama a class needs and how the teacher may provide them. The best illustration of this attitude towards teaching came from a pupil of the great Russian teacher and director of the Moscow Arts Theatre, Constantin Stanislavsky. She was illustrating the way Stanislavsky taught and said, 'The pupil must go shopping. It depends what recipe he is using, what pudding he wishes to make. The shopkeeper (the teacher) cannot force him to buy things that are not needed for the pudding. The shelves must be well stocked with helpful ingredients, but the customer can only carry home the items that he can make use of at that time.'

Definitions of drama

When meeting a class for the first time it is useful to talk briefly about what drama means.

It is often sadly true that a very experienced drama teacher may be so sure she knows what drama is (is for, is doing on the timetable, is about, and so on) that she can forget that, to a child, drama may mean something quite different.

In every society drama has a function to present our version of ourselves to ourselves, in a way that helps make sense of some little part of it. In our day and age this happens mostly through television, since in our society relatively few people congregate to share a dramatic experience. The theatre serves only a proportion of society for a proportion of the time. Television has made popular drama available to the majority, as the melodramas did in the nineteenth century.

Children, on being asked, 'What shall we do a play about?', may give answers based on their understanding of what drama is. They may say— a bank robbery—because that is the stuff of much cops and robbers television drama. They may quote the title of a programme which is popular. They may suggest a comedy programme. They may be influenced by the definition of a play as something they have seen—a Christmas pantomime or a schools' performance. They may have taken part in a school play themselves and been influenced by that concept of drama. They may have thought that drama in school is 'music and movement'. Less often they may think of drama as dramatic literature.

One class when asked why they thought drama was on the timetable said, 'In case any of us want to be actors, miss, so we'll know how to do it.' When asked if any of them might want to be an actor after leaving school these particular inner-city, twelve year old boys fell about laughing, because in their opinion actors were 'pouffs'!

It is unlikely that those particular boys would take drama seriously without a change of attitude. Also, since the room in which that lesson was scheduled to take place had a broken window, no furniture and a false ceiling above which pigeons were nesting, it was obvious that the school's low opinion of drama was equal to the boys'. If the teacher is going to raise the concept of drama to a level where it can be of value, then she is going to have to take cognizance of the pupil's understanding of drama before she begins.

It is not often that a teacher of any subject has to explain what that subject is before she can begin, but in drama the establishment of some common ground is useful in getting rid of misconceptions. It has often happened that, at the end of an exciting session when the children have been fully involved and ideas have been most productive, the class have said to the teacher, 'Can we do the play now?' simply because their idea of a play is of a performance on the stage, with the lights on and the curtains drawn between scenes. Much disappointment and frustration can be avoided if the teacher makes clear to the class what her definition of classroom drama is, whilst at the same time acknowledging the emphasis placed on certain kinds of activity by the pupils.

A group that is fascinated by form and structure and the techniques of presentation will merely be frustrated if they can never tackle the 'tricks of the trade'. Equally a class that is expert at the methods of presentation may be bored by a series of exercises in technique and may be looking for some meatier content or personal involvement.

The discussion about what drama means to the class and to the teacher, although vital to the succeeding lessons, should not exclude practical work in the very first class. It is easier to demonstrate, experiment and find out how the land lies in a practical way, as in the section on *Beginning the lesson*. The essential is to be open and honest about the nature of classroom drama in a way that is appropriate to the children and at a level at which the teacher feels confident of teaching it.

The teacher as an observer

Trying to pin down and analyse what is happening in a class is akin to the scientist's skill in appreciating a visual phenomenon and then making soundly based assumptions. So often the teacher is caught up in events in the classroom and cannot separate her own feelings from what is happening to her pupils.

Learning to 'read' one's class is as necessary as being confident in make-believe. There are some occasions when the emotional temperature in the class suggests that drama is already present to such a degree in their real-life situation, that anything that might fuel the tension could lead to explosion. The teacher sensing that situation might find it very profitable to release the emotion in some energetic, but uninvolved, exercise of movement or vocal technique that would dissipate the tension. Whatever the situation, being aware of the capabilities of the class, on that day, will allow for leeway in the lesson. No one should be held to a lesson plan, there is always another time, another day, when that lesson can be put into effect. Drama can only be handled effectively when the conditions are right. It is up to the teacher to determine what kind of drama the class is ready for and then to determine how to approach it.

It is possible to find oneself similarly confused by the degree of involvement or belief in the work of a class which one is observing from outside. That is one reason why teachers so often prefer to take a role in the drama and to keep the group together for at least part of the time, in order to test their emotional temperature. The skill here is in learning to leave one's own scale of values aside and judge merely what is being offered.

How can the teacher be sure that she is observing the signals correctly and so be able to choose the correct mode of work for her class? There are some assumptions that can safely be made, based on one's experience of children in general. A London teacher may find that the competitive quick-wittedness of inner-city children leads to a joky, facile glibness in their response to dramatic involvement and she will want to slow the drama down, while someone working in a less frenetic atmosphere may be striving for a quicker response. The non-committal attitude of the older 'academic' class in a school may be more difficult than the quarrelsome undisciplined third-year. But after the first assumption one must then rely on one's antennae to determine when to rein in and when to let go.

On one occasion a London teacher was asked to teach a class she had never met before in a school in Darlington. In order to plan the lesson it was necessary to make certain assumptions and certain guesses. How would the class react to a stranger? What would be of value to them in being taught by someone new? What sort of experience would be of most use to them? How should the lesson be paced in a way that would accommodate a period of getting acquainted? The teacher chose to examine the very area that seemed most problematical and so began the lesson by introducing herself as someone whom they might regard with no undue seriousness. She used her first name, she said she worked in a theatre, she talked about London as a place they might have visited—a tourist place, no more. This was so slight an exaggeration as to be not quite a role, more an extension of the physical and, most particularly, the vocal characteristics of an indolent, unimportant southerner. How did they view themselves in relation to a Londoner? Was their image of this stranger reflected in their image of themselves? This is where the teacher needed to use the 'antennae'. By questioning the class carefully she could assess their response. She asked what Darlington was famous for. The word 'famous' was carefully chosen to be in line with the role she had assumed—it was a somewhat fatuous word to use. The answer confirmed both the attitude she had suspected they might have of her as a southerner and of themselves as coming from the North East ... 'Railways'.

On hearing that one word the teacher knew she could proceed to elaborate on the relationship between herself representing 'London' and the class representing 'Darlington'. She led the questioning towards a demonstration of what railways meant to the town by a show of pretended ignorance, and the children demonstrated 'working'. The work was heavy, industrial work and one unexpected factor came into play. The girls' image of themselves was a very subordinate one. They saw themselves firmly allied to home and family and would only 'work' at cooking for the men.

By reading these signals the teacher then had to decide whether to take the class on to consider the traditional attitude they were demonstrating with regard to their own roles in life or to pursue the North vs. South attitude further. In a rather cowardly way she decided that the girls' role was probably too difficult a nut to crack and decided to involve them, if possible, in her original plan. She asked a group of girls if they would cook a meal in the works canteen and if she could hold a meeting there.

At the meeting she announced that the government in London had decided to withhold any further aid to industry in the North East unless it could be persuaded that their work was important. Was it important?

Since the only real objective this teacher had was to see if the attitude of North vs. South was a substantial one, her naive question was enough to raise an angry response. Without bothering with whether this was more than a cliché she encouraged the anger to grow into a protest march with slogans and chanting. The children took tambourines and drums and marched towards 'London'.

A sealed envelope had been planted in case it was needed. As the angry marchers came to Parliament (and the real dinner ladies came to lay the tables in the hall) this class received Lord Runciman's reply to the Jarrow Marchers, 'Go back and work out your own salvation'.

The decision to let the class go, in this case, was an easy one. The class was experienced and they had taken the path the teacher had guessed they might, but she had to read the signals about the way they saw their roles in relation to the way she had presented herself, in order to know how to proceed.

If there had been an opportunity to tackle the messages she was receiving about the girls' view of themselves she would then have to consider whether she was putting too much value on her own sense of women's role in society and interpreting their signals according to false or irrelevant standards of behaviour. Would it have been sensible to do a play with them about Ellen Wilkinson (who was Jarrow's M.P. and who marched to the House of Commons to present the petition)? Would this mean anything to the girls or would such a contrived attempt to raise their status be irrelevant to them and further evidence of the teacher's foreign attitude? But having observed the various responses to the test questions she had put to the class, the decision had to be made quickly, within the lesson itself. Sometimes the wrong decision is made, and the teacher then has to decide whether to stop the lesson or not. Sometimes it is only afterwards that it is possible to assess how much better it would have been to have taken another avenue. This is usually the moment to plan next week's lesson.

3

Introducing drama

The drama room: organizing space

Drama can happen anywhere: in a lift, in a cupboard, sitting in a chair. However, classroom drama does have certain elements about it which suggest an ideal teaching space.

In the first place, drama work can be noisy. This is not to say that it is always noisy. Many head teachers are justly afraid of drama because they have come to associate it with seemingly undisciplined behaviour in the school hall. However, even at its best, any group of children moving about and talking can be disturbing to other groups who are sitting in silence, so an ideal drama room is one where a certain amount of noise can be tolerated.

Secondly, there is the question of floor area. The huge open spaces of the school hall can be very disturbing to concentrated work and can often suggest the wrong sort of associations—wet playtime or indoor games, performances on the stage, school assembly or the setting up of tables for lunch. If the hall is the best place available, then the teacher must plan how to bring the children in to a working atmosphere, so that these other associations will not be distracting. If the teacher puts herself in the place of a pupil in that class and thinks, 'What do I need to make me feel comfortable and able to work in a concentrated way?', she will probably find that there are some further questions that need careful consideration, such as: Do the class need to assemble outside the room and prepare themselves? Where in the school have they come from? What kind of lesson has preceded this one? What is the weather like? Are they used to sitting on the floor or do they regard chairs as necessary? Are their shoes appropriate? Where should they put their belongings? Do they like each other? Do the boys and the girls work together?

Having run through this sort of check-list the teacher can then arrange her teaching space accordingly. If there are severe limits on time and space, drama can be tailored to a classroom with desks. A group of children in wheelchairs can be just as adept as any other, but the physical surroundings are so important that they must be seriously thought out and taken into account.

A drama studio is sometimes available, and although specific trappings such as lighting, sound reproducing equipment, paints, dressing up clothes, make-up and rostra are all useful at some time, they can be a distraction. Some classes are so conditioned to think of drama in terms of equipment that they cannot work without it. This has more serious disadvantages than often appear at first sight. Since drama is a 'fictional' occupation it is concerned with what happens in the imagination. This is then conveyed from one member of the group to another by means of words, physical attitudes, expression and gesture. If imagination is limited by the necessity of finding something to represent a sword or a kitchen stove and this 'something' has either to be the real thing or has to be accepted by the rest of the group as a suitable symbol, then at the least, time is wasted in selecting the most appropriate object; at the worst, the participants must stand outside the drama, waiting for imagination to take over again. Small children in imaginative play do this all the time: 'Pretend this is a car and I'm the driver'. However, in class work, the amount of hassle over arranging blocks to form a shop may lead away from the imaginative pursuit of an idea about shortage of food.

The teacher needs to consider the value of using real objects and to help the class establish the habit of working from imagination without either needing to use real objects or theatrical devices as a stimulus when no performance is envisaged or they do not promote the drama in any way.

On the other hand the teacher may plan to use a theatrical device such as lighting or music as the basis of the lesson. All that is necessary is to realize the part that such an element will play in the structuring of the lesson from the children's point of view. There is further detail on equipment in the section on *Resources*, and at the end of the chapter on *Beginning the lesson*.

The lesson plan

Many would-be teachers of drama consider that it is not necessary to plan a lesson beforehand. This is often the result of having watched very experienced drama teachers who seem to have no plan worked out in advance and who appear to place themselves purely at the disposal of the class. What is not clear is that such teachers have a deep well of former experience to draw from and are thus able to go along with the class while at the same time possessing the resources to change the direction of the drama if such change is necessary.

For most of us, a lesson plan is an essential lifeline. In fact it is often useful to have two lessons planned, one as an alternative, in case conditions are not right.

By adopting the methods of the fictional models on page 8 we can see that the lesson plan does not need to set out the plot of the drama or the story of the play, because this can be left to develop during the lesson. It is also quite possible that if an idea or theme appeals to a class it may well extend itself over several lessons. What should be at the heart of any lesson plan is the one single objective that the teacher has isolated as important from her observation of the class. It has nothing to do with subject matter, it is solely concerned with the development of the ability to understand human behaviour a little better by sharing in the playing-out of some aspects of it. What the teacher needs to do is to select the most appropriate aspect and shape her lesson towards that end. Sometimes this objective can be a very limited one. It could be something related to the pupils' own classroom behaviour. One teacher spent four weeks on 'learning not to hit each other' which is a limited version of 'learning to respect other people's opinions' ... It could be that the teacher wishes to pinpoint one aspect of the character of King Lear, but the underlying area that she wants the class to experience is what it is like to be a parent. Whatever her objective may be she will have to plan her lesson so that the class can achieve satisfaction by involving themselves in something that is well within their grasp whilst allowing them to look at the wider issues and extend their range of understanding.

Having selected an objective the teacher then needs to choose an appropriate context, that is the 'setting' for the drama. This is where most of the planning needs to take place, since the choice of an appropriate context determines so much. It will have to be interesting enough in itself to hold the class's attention, it will have to provide a focus for the objective the teacher has selected, it will have to be suitable for a manageable group to inhabit and it must be sufficiently concrete and realistic to allow a serious attitude to develop. By setting the play in an environment such as an old people's home, a remote village or a railway station, one is suggesting that, although the place seems real enough, the people that are found there bear no resemblance to the actors themselves. Establishing a fictional setting gives a greater security to the participant in the drama. As in the case of the classic examples quoted earlier, the children are transported into another world of experience. Asking children to reproduce their own life style is like reading their private diaries. It usually produces caricature and comedy send-ups as an evasion of reality, or it produces acceptable stereotypes of the 'family at breakfast' variety. The moment when a group will *offer* something of their own experience should be treasured by the teacher as a measure of the trust that exists between them. It is not something that should ever be demanded or regarded as a matter of right.

Having chosen a suitable context for the drama the teacher will now have to plan the right approach. Sometimes there will need to be a number of 'run-ups' to the main target area. The class may not be ready to go straight into the play without having something easy to start on, to increase their confidence and to get into a way of working. It is also sometimes necessary to quieten a class and to focus their thinking. The teacher will have to decide what is the best approach when she meets the class. It is as well to have several ploys in hand.

Having planned the approach run, the teacher will probably be able to start the play itself quite simply. It may be useful to rehearse over to oneself the exact words with which to begin the drama. This is particularly true if one is starting the play in role, as it is important to find the right emotional temperature to start with: too high and the class may be frightened off, too low and they may not become involved at all. (See section on *Teaching in role*.)

It is not usually very helpful to plan further than the setting up of the drama, since the class itself will probably determine the direction they wish the play to go. The teacher, however, will certainly want to do two more things at least before going to the lesson. She will want to plan at least one possible device to increase the group's commitment to the drama, in case they are working on too facile a level to satisfy their own needs; and she will want to know how to round off the lesson. As experience increases in both the class and the teacher, these can be left unplanned, but at first she will need to plan for a satisfactory amount of time for discussion and reflection at the end of the lesson and, if the class is excitable, a time for cooling off before going to their next lesson. The primary teacher is at a distinct advantage since she is more likely to be able to control her own timetable, but nevertheless a satisfactory ending is very important and needs to be planned into the timing of the lesson.

Control factors and teaching techniques

The sort of nightmare which can make one wake up in a cold sweat is that of the drama lesson which has got out of control. Because drama concerns a large group of people in a 'dramatic' situation, it can very easily topple over into chaos. This is in part why drama is not easy to teach and is also why it has sometimes got a bad reputation in schools.

If we analyse the reasons why drama sometimes gets out of hand it should be easier to establish controls. In the first place, the normal classroom structure does not apply to drama, the relationship between pupil and teacher is different. Secondly, the teacher is encouraging rather than repressing verbal and physical responses. Finally, the raw material of drama is sometimes emotionally high-pitched.

Sometimes teachers make things unduly difficult by including as necessary factors in drama 1) a degree of conflict and 2) an absence of teacher interference, both of which can be very difficult for the class to handle in a constructive way. Conflict may be essential for a well-written play, it may also very occasionally provide an important ingredient in classroom drama, but it should rarely, if ever, be used to divide a group. The conflict is best seen as happening between the group and outside forces, even if those forces are represented only by 'messages' or by the teacher (see *Lesson 3: Life in the trenches*). Whether to intervene is sometimes difficult to judge successfully, but if the teacher is already participating in the drama it is much easier to control the rise of undue excitement in her pupils and to allow greater emotional risks to be taken, than if she has to come in from outside and spoil the spontaneity.

As well as looking for the reasons for *loss* of control it is as well to look for the advantages of working in a controlled situation. Apart from safety factors there are several other good reasons why drama needs to be firmly controlled. The class should be given a sense of security, of knowing that anger, distress, excitement, fear and other emotions may come to the top during the drama and that a seemingly real feeling can flood through the individual taking part, and can not only be felt, but actually savoured, because the situation is not real. If there is total security about the way the lesson is conducted, all this emotional energy can be harnessed in a way that is cathartic and beneficial. Without a secure basis it can become too real and the children may draw back and produce nothing but superficial work or, on the other hand, actual 'real' violence may break out leading to fights and squabbling.

Another reason for firm control by the teacher is her own survival in the classroom. All teaching is tiring; drama teaching is by its very nature particularly exhausting, because it involves so many different kinds of response. In order to minimize wear and tear the teacher must be able to maintain a level of control which she finds comfortable.

Serious attitudes
There are various ways in which the teacher can devise her own control systems. The most effective, however, is not a series of 'dos and don'ts', but a firmly established attitude towards drama generally. If the teacher takes her own and her pupils' work seriously from the outset, then a positive attitude is more likely to be established. Because drama is enjoyable, and because it is so obviously allied in many people's minds to 'childish' pursuits like pretending and playing games, it is very easy for everyone concerned to take drama lightly, as just a piece of fun. Teachers sometimes contribute to this feeling by showing a flippant attitude, by tending to use a large number of games in their lessons and by encouraging a superficial approach, allowing what a child says or does to be regarded as funny, because it may be accidentally anachronistic or inappropriate.

Because drama is an activity which involves the whole person, there is often a heightened sensitivity towards himself and others in every individual taking part. This means that things done or said as part of the drama will be spontaneous and offered in a spirit of excitement. Personal criticism or, even worse, laughter, can be very hurtful and can lead to a refusal on the part of that individual to become involved to any depth ever again.

It is often the pupil with the most delicate self-esteem who finds drama difficult. At any age, the boy or girl who is struggling to establish identity or to find a level among his or her peers may not wish to submit to a pretence where he or she may lose face. The level of involvement of even the most dedicated drama student can vary from moment to moment. This means that the teacher needs to preserve a serious atmosphere surrounding what is happening in the classroom, so that nobody is likely to feel that delicately balanced relationships with peers are at risk.

Real time and dramatic time

Taking drama slowly is another way of establishing control. By watching television plays, especially plays which contain a great deal of action, the viewer may be led to suppose that everything happens at an increased rate. There are a number of short scenes and whole days (and nights) can be indicated by short, 'significant' pieces of action. When making their own drama, the group will often want to do the same. It will be a part of the shorthand that they regard as necessary, usually being unaware of the process of selection that has produced those pieces of action rather than any other, in the television play.

If the teacher can help a class to get rid of the idea that classroom drama is in any way the same as television drama, and can lead the group to concentrate on exploring one situation in depth, rather than following a narrative pattern, then she can slow down the passage of time to a more realistic level.

This is where it becomes very necessary for the teacher herself to sort out what kind of drama she wants in her classroom and to encourage her class to broaden their ideas about what drama involves. Thus it is probably necessary to set out a few rules for the conduct of classroom drama which when practised will help to establish the nature of the activity.

Rules for drama

These rules have to depend on the physical surroundings and on the teacher's tolerance level, but some statement of intent is useful to the pupils, as well as being a quiet way of beginning the lesson. (See page 12). Before any work can start, the class has to come to rest and signify their readiness to begin. Many teachers have found it useful to have their pupils make a circle of chairs (or sit on the floor in a circle). This arrangement is not only democratic, it is also a traditional theatre form and highly appropriate. The teacher can then use that resting position to make clear everything that needs to be said by:

1   Using the word 'work' fairly often, thus encouraging the class to think of drama as a serious matter.
2   Explaining exactly what is under consideration and making sure that the class understands what is expected of them.

3 Ensuring by demonstration and by experiment that the class understands how they and the teacher will work together.
4 Showing and explaining that everyone will take part and that usually there will be nobody watching.
5 Making sure that everyone knows about 'forbidden' areas of the room (if there are hidden difficulties, such as a curtained-off stage).
6 Discussing quietly what the class and the teacher are looking for in terms of classroom drama.

Most of these rules do not need to be stated aloud more than once, if at all. Teachers may have many more of their own that they wish to add; but beginning with some convention such as sitting in a circle or 'finding a space' is fairly usual, as is also some way of signalling that the teacher wishes the activity to stop.

Working from inside the play as one of the participants makes stopping it relatively easy (see *Teaching in role*). The use of some loud instrument such as a tambour or cymbal, seems to suggest that the level of noise is going to be unnecessarily high. It also seems very obtrusive to cut off activity in such a bad-mannered and abrupt way. Devising a set of visual signals with the class would seem more productive. 'We can let the play go on until we find out more about why people may want to leave the country they were born in, and then when we think we've done enough, I will go and sit by the piano and you can come and join me and we can talk about what we've done. I should think that would be about twelve o'clock.'

This way of establishing a method of working is obviously a very personal one, but the teacher needs to make the parameters clear, for her own and the class's security.

Control devices
1 *Being able to stop*
This involves, for example, the ability to say 'All right, we've seen how the family coped with that bit of the problem, now what would happen if we looked ahead a bit...'

This means that teacher and class can assess what has taken place so far and can look for greater depth, either by going forward or backward in time. It also allows several other things to happen. In the first place, the class is not having to cope with shaping or tightening its own work by finding a climax or ending, at the same time as wrestling with ideas, words, and unfamiliar situations. Secondly, they can more clearly distinguish between the 'as if' (the fiction) and the 'here and now' (the reality). Thirdly, they can have a rest and pause for relaxation and reflection, and finally the teacher can exert some influence, so helping the class to extend its work without being critical or seeming to interfere.

2 *Changing the activity*

Depending on the length of the lesson, the teacher either can allow a long, slow build-up to some kind of conclusion, or will have to calculate on getting the most out of several shorter pieces of work. This also depends on how much the class is able to concentrate and how much confidence they have to plunge into a longish piece of drama. A sequence of short, easily managed activities may be more helpful at some stage, while the class is learning how to work together on something more extending. Writing and drawing can be built in to the lesson (a letter home, a plan of the house, etc.), as can looking at photographs or a picture, listening to the teacher narrating the story (as in *Lesson 1: The Cavalry*), and listening to or reading a passage which expresses the ideas they have worked on. Many different activities can be used, wherever a change is felt necessary in order to re-focus attention or sharpen perception.

3 *Practising*

This is not the same thing as rehearsing. What is meant by practising is that the teacher (in role) suggests that the characters in the play should practise some event which might be important in the future. For example, since the soldiers are obviously not going to be able to fight the war which is becoming more and more important in the play they are engaged on, there may be very good reasons for suggesting that they 'practise' fighting an imaginary enemy. The same thing can be used as a way of ensuring that some future part of the play will not be held up for want of information. The important meeting with the king can be practised beforehand so that the villagers have sorted out their own priorities. This can also be helpful in building belief as well as giving a measure of control over events. (See *Chapter 5* for further details on building belief.)

4 *Narrating*

The teacher can often narrate a piece of action which could prove too difficult for the class to handle. She can use narrative as a device to give form and structure to an otherwise rather loosely or carelessly worked out piece of drama or sequence of short episodes. It can also serve to move on a piece of work which is becoming bogged down in detail, or in danger of being sidetracked.

5 *'Freezing', slow motion, 'still photographs', mimed activity*

These are all ways in which a class can be helped to slow down or remain still and quiet for a minute. They also help to focus on an important moment in the play and either enable the class to pick up where they left off or to hold something in their minds for future reference. (A Polaroid camera which produces a *real* photograph can be a useful tool in recording an important event for the next lesson.)

6 *Looking for form*

This is not simply a control device, it is an alternative way of looking at the drama lesson. In a lesson which is concerned to build up the pupils' involvement and total belief in a given situation it can be salutary to suggest that the class draw back for a moment and give some kind of form to what they have done. The teacher might say, 'I wonder how those explorers could make the rest of the world understand what they felt when they came into the city and found it deserted. Suppose we acted it out again in a way that *anyone* could understand.' This provides a chance to re-focus a moment in the play which may almost have slipped by, because class and teacher were not ready for it. There is a good deal to be said for encouraging a class to spend time on finding ways to approach a problem from a new angle. 'Supposing this were a scene in a film, how would it be different?' 'How would a newspaper reporter be likely to regard the events in that street? Let's set it up, and see.' Fixing the important events by re-playing them can also be a way of starting off the next lesson. A scene that was 'fixed' at the end of the previous session can be re-run at the beginning of the next, to serve as a reminder and a starting point.

7 *Grouping*

Whilst it is obviously most satisfactory that everyone in the room is engaged in the same play at the same time, it sometimes happens that the children are not happy working in this way in which case the lesson can be planned to include individual work, work in pairs, in groups of three or four, and so on. In a mixed school it sometimes happens that boys and girls will not work together and it often happens that for some reason an individual or small group is unpopular and no one wants to work with them. The teacher has to decide whether it is worth forcing the issue or whether to allow time to elapse for the matter to sort itself out. In many cases the problem is solved by setting up a situation which involves everyone in the room and leaving the members of the group to make contact as they please. If the content is interesting and the belief strong enough, the drama should prove more enthralling than the other problems.

It is sometimes the case that the strong boy/girl split, which is part of growing up, can be used as an issue in the drama, as in *Lesson 2: The Tribe*. This, however, is very much a matter for the individual teacher to decide. One cannot make drama the solution to every social problem within the group, even though it can and often should concern itself with these very issues, and help to throw them into some kind of relief.

Beginning the lesson

Since setting the right tone is so vitally important, the most important lesson of all is going to be the one when teacher and class first meet, because this will be the moment where they establish 1) the nature of the subject; 2) the method of working; 3) the relationship that will exist in future.

It is for this reason that other essential things like learning the names of the pupils may be left to another occasion. There may not be enough time to achieve even the three objectives listed above, let alone any more; therefore, let us assume that the idea is to conduct a lesson which will serve as a sample, so that the class and the teacher know exactly what they are letting themselves in for.

A sample lesson

The class form a circle (preferably on chairs, with the teacher as part of the circle); the teacher introduces herself and explains that they are going to do some drama, and that everyone in the circle will be in the play. She says that she will begin several short plays by pretending to be someone other than herself.

The first 'play' is simply a piece of mimed activity where the teacher goes outside the circle by moving her chair, thus creating an 'entrance'. She then comes in to the space and mimes something like hanging out some washing or changing the wheel of a car. She then returns to her seat and sits back in the circle. This basic activity does several things: 1) it establishes dramatic activity without using real objects; 2) it establishes the activity rather than the 'character'; 3) the children's function is momentarily that of an audience; 4) it makes it possible to establish that the end of any play will be indicated by the teacher sitting in her chair again. This will also serve for other sessions in the future.

The teacher then asks the class to guess what she was doing. This is obviously so easy that there are no traps, no hidden difficulty, but someone other than the teacher is going to have to speak. Then the question is elaborated into a query about what else we now know about the situation: whether it seemed to be windy or wet, whether the car driver knew about changing wheels, and so on. Here the objective is to accept those contributions based on real observation and to query others. 'Do we really *know* that by what the woman did, or do you think she might be the sort of person who *might* do that in the future, because we ought to be sure?' It is important, even in such a simple exercise, that the class become used to extracting information from what they see and hear and not inventing wildly and improbably. In future lessons the ability to take seriously what is offered as information during the drama is going to be crucial. On the other hand, the teacher can establish that all comment is going to be taken at face value. Any flippant replies are going to be subjected to scrutiny. All this may have taken relatively few minutes. It is then time to pass on to the next stage, which is to ask the children to join in. This is not done formally. The teacher simply points out how much they have found out as a result of a play lasting only a few seconds. She now says she will begin another play which will be rather longer, but which will begin in the same way.

She moves the chair back and begins to mime carrying a crate of milk bottles and puts one 'bottle' down in front of a child she has already identified as an uninhibited member of the group. Looking the child straight in the eye she begins, 'Good morning, Mrs Jones (or Mr Jones), I can't remember if it was today you wanted an extra pint.' Mrs Jones may reply in the affirmative, the negative, or just by giggling, but the teacher will press the conversation a little further, perhaps talking about the intended visitors which were the cause of her ordering extra milk. She will then pass on to another 'customer', perhaps Mr Brown, who is unexpectedly home from work. Depending on the length of the response, the teacher might go on to ask Mr Brown whether old Mr (or Mrs) Green was home from the hospital after his accident—she would then pass on to where Mr Green 'lived' and call out to determine whether he was all right.

Returning to the teacher's chair and so ending the play, the teacher can then question the whole class as to what they have learned about Mrs Jones, Mr Brown and Mr Green, repeating the technique of being precise about what is known and what may be assumed. The teacher also asks the class what they know about 'the person I was pretending to be'. The class usually reply, 'You were a milkman, miss'. This provokes some useful discussion on another simple but vital factor—the teacher is a woman, but they assumed that it was a milkman not a milk-lady, because where they come from milk is delivered by men. This is fundamental to the business of establishing that taking a role in a play is purely a matter of who you say you are, or what you do. The class also establish that a role *can* be given to someone simply by saying 'Good morning, Mrs Jones', but that usually people choose to be the sort of person that suits them best.

The teacher summarizes the kind of building up of information that has already happened by drawing attention to the fact that instead of knowing the story beforehand, we find out what the story is, little by little, as we get further into the play. She then asks if they would like to try to do another one which could last longer and could involve every-body. Usually by this time they are eager to try.

The teacher removes her chair again and picks up a notepad and pencil. She begins the play by saying, 'Ladies and gentlemen, we're very grateful that so many of the people who saw the accident, when the little boy was knocked down, could come here this evening to give evidence. How many of you actually saw the car?' Hands go up. The teacher questions an individual. 'Yes, sir, could I have your name and address please ... Well, Mr Samuels, perhaps you wouldn't mind just describing what you were doing when you saw the car ... How fast do you think it was going? ... Did anyone else happen to notice the number? ... Your name, Madam? ... and so on, bringing in as many children as possible, but allowing them to offer information voluntarily for the most part and encouraging them to create their own characters.

The teacher tries not to allow too many contradictions by repeating the main facts: 'Is there someone here who was on the same side as the bus driver and who saw this blue car?' She may also involve the class in a minimum of physical action by beginning to draw a map on the blackboard or asking a witness to demonstrate where he was standing relative to the action.

This may be enough for the first lesson, but if there is time the teacher might well include a further stage of the same play by suggesting that the witnesses coordinate parts of the story. This depends on what has emerged from the information given, but it might be that those people who saw the masked men park the car and transfer to another car should act out what they saw, with the teacher talking them through the episode.

Anyway, whatever happens, there must be time for a return to the circle and a resumé, out of role, of what kind of drama has happened in that lesson. The teacher will point out any difficult passages where perhaps someone introduced a red herring which made it hard to maintain belief and she will reinforce the importance of building a play slowly, using only the resources available, emphasizing how much has been discovered about people and places. She would also, if it were her own class and she had time, probably ask for a further piece of work based on the drama; a map or a piece of written evidence, a newspaper report. This helps give drama some further significance for children who may still think of it as a rather pointless pastime. Not that it is *always* a good thing to give written work to justify drama. It carries its own justification; but on this occasion the teacher might want to get as much value from the children's contribution as possible in order to give it importance in their eyes, as an invention which became concrete enough to write about or pin down in the form of a map.

During this first lesson, the level of excitement has not been high and hardly anyone has left his or her seat. Also, the teacher has done most of the work and kept the reins firmly in her own hands. Certainly this will not be the level of subsequent lessons, but as a sample it has established a number of principles which should prove useful later on, and it has served as a taster for future lessons in a way which has avoided lengthy explanations.

Other beginnings to other lessons

The objective of the sample lesson was to give an idea of classroom drama to a class which does not know the teacher and has not tried drama of this sort before.

The planned approach to a lesson must take into account the objective which the teacher has selected, but there are some well-tried starters which could be used as further sample lessons to introduce a class to a way of working, and which have as their objective establishing the idea of a common suspension of disbelief.

1 *Discussion*

This involves discussing a topic to find out those areas which would be most suitable to be worked on dramatically. The great value of starting with a short discussion is that it eliminates the idea that you have to 'do the whole play'. Therefore, the class can concentrate on an in-depth exploration of just one area.

Suppose, for example, that a topical news items about a strike had been chosen. The class could suggest possible aspects to be worked on and the teacher could list them. This could easily result in enough work for several lessons, although spinning a topic out endlessly may result in the class becoming bored with it and does not take into account the teacher's objectives for the development of the class as a group.

Taking one aspect of the topic that appeals to the majority of the class, the teacher may suggest that they work in role, all together, and that she should take part, giving herself a role such as shop steward or convener (which would enable her to start the play off and draw the class in, much the same as her role as policeman did in the road accident play).

If the class is more experienced, then the teacher may suggest a way of working on their own, in groups. They could try out some smaller situation such as a family conference, which might pin-point some of the effects of the strike on workers' families.

2 *Working backwards*

This involves starting with the climax of some action: a photograph or article from a newspaper, a scene from a TV play enacted by some of the class, a short excerpt from a play text or novel. The class then takes the story back in stages by setting up an imaginary situation which might have preceded the one illustrated. By this means they can follow the characters back in a chain of motivation to find out how it all began. The teacher acts as director and the scenes are probably very short. There is a good deal of discussion. This is a method that suits a rather intellectual class who might regard drama as 'playing'.

3 *Establishing identity*

This can be achieved by working on some occupational mime which allows a group to establish the reality of both occupation and group identity. This is probably more useful with younger children who are nearer to the 'playing house' type of dramatic activity. There are occasions where it can be used to establish the reality of a situation with older children but this is usually more in the nature of clarifying the setting for a play, such as working in a factory, having the family meal, or tea at the old folk's home (which has been mentioned already).

4 *Opening lines*

Here the aim is to get a class used to fluency in following a lead in an improvised situation. This is useful where a class, especially of older students, may repeatedly block the growth of a situation by introducing too much conflict. Trying out a number of useful opening lines suggested by the class, in order to see what directions the plays could move in, is one way of flexing dramatic muscle. Another way is for the teacher to use a clearly defined role and a carefully thought out opener, to begin a play which can then grow and develop in any one of a possible number of directions.

Some suggestions may be of help to teachers in thinking out their own examples.

1   'How can you be sure none of you were followed?'
2   'I bring greetings from my chief in this time of trouble.'
3   'Is it safe for me to join you?'
4   'How many do you think they'll allow us to send through the gate?'

Most opening lines take the form of questions but there is an art to questioning which needs practice. Experienced teachers of other subjects get used to framing questions in a way which allows only one 'correct' answer. In drama, questions have to be framed to allow the widest range of response, often in the form of other questions. If the teacher finds herself getting 'yes' or 'no' in reply, then she knows she'll have to think again, or amplify her question.

The third question in the list above requires a 'yes' or 'no' answer, but it also has implications for the people who answer it and much may depend on the response. Here the teacher is allowing the class to dictate the context of the play.

The first and second questions have quite clear connotations for the class to catch on to. The fourth has a more complex set of surrounding factors. Depending on the age of the class, they may interpret 'gate' in different ways.

6 *Visual aids*

Objects, maps, documents, announcements, can all be used to spark off drama. Although, generally speaking, real objects are a hindrance rather than a help, starting off with a significant prop can stimulate the imagination. A good many plays can be started by using the role of a foreign explorer who has a rudimentary map and needs help to exploit the territory (further implications for the group to develop). Notices of slave auctions, pieces of 'bone', a plastic bag of 'clues', a symbolic 'chain of

office', a 'crown', or similar important-looking object can serve to introduce a role to a group and eke out an opening gambit in some way. They
do not have to be real. Theatrical props and fake papers are just as good.

7 *Movement*

A more conventional way of starting a lesson is to build up a sequence of
movement exercises dictated by the teacher, each one intended to lead in
to the next and where the final one is designed to be a run-up to the play
itself. An example of such a sequence might be:

1   Movement work concentrating on the feet.
2   Walking on the spot.
3   Walking through shallow water.
4   Wading through water to the knees, the hips, the armpits, 'feel-
    ing' the weight and pressure of the body through the current.
5   The group is fording a river. What awaits them on the other
    side? Can they get across by helping each other?

8 *Music*

Many teachers like to use music as a stimulus to dramatic activity. This
book is, however, largely concerned with language-based drama and not
with either dance or movement, except where movement is part of the
drama. This is why music is not regarded as particularly fruitful on its
own as a starter, although it may be used to accompany part of the
activity or as an aid to the more reflective parts of a lesson. One example
of the use of music could be a storm sequence played during the writing
of an account of an Atlantic crossing in an immigrant ship. Other teachers
may find music useful if they want to start with a sequence of exercises or
a movement sequence leading into drama work.

9 *Games*

As mentioned before, the over-use of drama games is a way of avoiding
drama, rather than a way into drama. However, the occasional individual game that precedes the opening of the play itself may be all that is
needed to bring a group into a state of preparedness to begin.

10 *Role play exercises*

There are many ways of setting up such exercises. The following may
serve as an example. The class works in pairs, A and B. A tells B what he
did at the weekend. This is done as himself. Then B takes the role of A's
parent and A tells the story again. Does it differ? Now B takes the role of
a police officer who is taking down a statement about what A did during
the weekend. B is trying to cross-question A about his story. Has A's story
altered? What are their respective attitudes towards each other? Is the
story now 'true' in the same sense that it was 'true' in the beginning?

11 *Simulation exercises, role cards, etc.*

For desk-bound classes and the more inhibited older groups who find drama embarrassing these provide a good way to begin. There are a number of excellent manufactured simulation exercises on the market. It is also very possible to create one's own, using either a central problem and allocating roles which have a declared interest to students who will then prepare their 'case' for a public debate; or a 'case-study' type of simulation where the debate involves characters related to the central, absent, case-study character. Students often find it helpful to work in groups representing different points of view.

Useful material is often found in social studies publications as well as in the reports of court cases in newspapers. It is perhaps wiser not to choose local examples and the courtroom formula itself is probably less useful than the rather more informal debate or enquiry, as the class can become very enmeshed in the details of legal procedure. The personal nature of the involvement, however, can be highly charged and very productive, even with a class firmly rooted in desks. As a general rule the style of work produced as a result of using such formal procedures as simulation packs is nearer to debate than to drama. Nevertheless, they do provide a way in which an older but inexperienced group may gain confidence and realize that drama is not as daunting as they had first believed.

More lessons can lead on from this beginning point using a 'going back in time' technique, exploring some of the circumstances which led up to the enquiry, in order to find out more about the people involved.

4

Strategies

Teaching in role

Teaching in role is the technique by which the teacher takes part in the drama herself, thus enabling her to manoeuvre from within the activity, without having to exert authority from outside.

The advantages are clearly those of being able to perceive more immediately what is going on, of being accepted as someone who does not know all the answers (and therefore relies on the group to work even harder to provide solutions), of being able to challenge, question and slow down the activity by preventing the group from skipping over serious issues.

The difficulties lie in the initial reluctance of the teacher to expose herself by 'acting' or pretending in front of the class, and in the reluctance of the class to accept the teacher in any other than the traditional pedagogic function.

If we accept that to be successful, drama is a shared activity, then for the teacher to join in can only enhance the notion of sharing, experimenting and analysing the work in hand. The presence of anyone watching what is going on, when the group is engaging itself in believing in the 'Big Lie', is bound to be distracting. An audience of any kind is only useful when it is employed by the teacher or group to fulfil a particular function, such as fixing the action or trying to find some form for the drama. Therefore even an audience of one—the teacher—suggests to many children that they may be 'doing it wrong' or that they have to look as though they are busily 'acting' when they are really not involved in any way.

At first an inexperienced class may not find it easy to accept the idea of a teacher working in role. Many teachers say that the children only giggle and do not take it seriously. Introducing this technique implies so much that is new and different in the class/teacher relationship that it needs to be approached gradually. The class may want to try some role-play exercises. The teacher may also use some kind of bridge between her traditional function with a class and the function that the role has in the play. For example, the role may be the best way of starting off a play, in which case she may have a brief discussion with the class about the play they are going to do and then say something like 'I'm going to go to the other end of the room. When I come back I shall be speaking not as myself but as someone else and the play will have begun.' This means that the teacher is simply representing the attitude of mind of the person she has chosen. That person will, in turn, represent some function which will be useful to the play.

Teaching in role is not acting. An actor's job is to put all the individuality he can find into a character so that he becomes not just any gate-keeper, but one specific gate-keeper with a set of personal characteristics and idiosyncracies. During intensive drama-work a class may want to move towards achieving that sort of skill, especially in presenting plays to other people, but teaching in role is not at all the same thing. The role is selected to serve a function: it is a teaching tool and not a particular 'character'.

Selecting a role to serve a teaching function needs careful thought; it will depend to a large extent on the roles that the teacher wants her class to adopt. Having decided what she hopes her class will learn from this session, she will then choose a category of roles for them—for example, people who need to rebel. She will choose a context—a strict regime or feudal village. Then she will choose her own role. Whatever facet of learning she chooses to explore, her role will need to be the one which best allows her to fulfil that function. If she feels that the class needs to band together to face authority and feel their own power, she may represent that authority herself as the feudal lord and take all their anger on herself by challenging them to attack her verbally. She may want them to question the rights of those in authority and so look at some of the possible reasons for repressive measures, in which case she may choose to represent the point of view of the anarchist or John Ball. Or she may want the class to move very slowly and gently, to feel the comfort of total order and mindless obedience and so she will choose the role of the lord's man, and so on, ad infinitum.

Whatever the function of the role, by saying that she will represent or speak as that person the teacher emphasizes that it is the thinking that is important, not whether the person looks old or young, has a wooden leg or speaks with a foreign accent. The thinking may, however, imply the presence of some such aspect. For example, it may be very important that the person the teacher represents is known to be old (representative of established thinking?) or invalid (helpless and requiring to be considered?) or a foreigner (needing to be instructed?) because such factors may affect the thinking of the group. All that is necessary is for the teacher to *mention* that she is old. She does not need to represent it in action by assuming the posture of an old woman. Nevertheless the attitudes represented by the role will probably affect the tone of voice and the words used by the teacher whilst she is in role. It is difficult to lay down any guidelines for this, it is a matter of personal choice. Some teachers 'characterize' speech more than others. It is certainly useful to be able to denote the moment when one is in role and the times when the role has been dropped and the drama is over. It is also helpful to the class, in moving into role themselves, if a different style of language is being used by the teacher. The same thing applies to body language. A commanding stance and a formal style takes the class straightaway into a certain mode, whereas a helpless wringing of the hands, nervous eye-movements and short, broken sentences help to produce a quite different response. All this is so much a matter of inclination on the part of the individual teacher that she has to work out her own pattern of what she and the class can accept.

It may be really useful to use more than one role during the play. For instance the teacher may feel the need to start off with a role that allows her to behave, within the play, very much according to the normal teacher/pupil relationship. She will then probably choose a role which carries authority with it, such as: the leader of the gang, the king, the wise woman, the elder, the foreman, etc. Later in the same play she may want to stop and start again with some new aspect, and this time she may choose an enquiring role: a stranger, a reporter, an apprentice, a herald. All that is usually necessary is for the teacher to introduce herself in a few words. 'Excuse me, I'm a stranger here. Can you give me a moment to rest and to hear your news?' This lets the class know not only who the teacher is representing but also what attitude they are expected to have. (Do they allow a stranger in when she obviously needs help, but wants to know what they are doing?)

Sometimes it is not even necessary to change the role in order to change gear in the lesson. The same role may have second thoughts, a seemingly mild townswoman may, during the council meeting, suddenly lose patience with those who are about to sweep through some measures over the heads of a rather weak opposition and will come down heavily on the side of the oppressed, thereby throwing a degree of weight into the scales and challenging, perhaps, the normal authority of some members of the class who usually have things all their own way.

Because roles are considered for their teaching function and not for their feasibility as acting parts, such things as the sex of the role become irrelevant, as in the example of the milkman quoted earlier.

A class may, however, quite easily accept the woman teacher as a king, whilst refusing to visualize a male teacher as a mother. If there is any likelihood of the teacher's choice being unacceptable, or if embarrassment results from the class's refusal to see the teacher in such a role, then it is probably wiser to stop and discuss the problem, although some teachers have got away with a blunt remark such as, 'I see you think there's something odd about the way I look, but I can't help that. What are you going to do about my baby?' It is the degree of belief which makes a role acceptable and it is wise to establish that at an early stage.

One of the advantages of working in role is that one can say things as the person who represents a certain attitude, which one could not say as a teacher. In role the language can be forceful and provocative and can challenge a vigorous response that might not be regarded as proper between teacher and pupil. One can also play the devil's advocate, just as one can extend the pupil's language by adopting a highly formal style.

It may be found that in certain circumstances the class will give the teacher a role, either formally by asking if she will act in a particular function, or informally by saying, 'Are you the owner of this horse?' If in this case the play had begun with everyone working at loading goods on to a ship, the teacher would have to consider whether that role would allow her enough room to influence the conduct of the drama. Sometimes it is possible to go along with the way the class has cast you. Sometimes it is just as important to stop and discuss it, as one would discuss any other casting which looked difficult. It could be that the whole play is affected by the casting of just one person—not necessarily the teacher. Casting a very diffident child in the role of emperor, perhaps with the support of the teacher as a lord chamberlain, might have very positive results, both for the child and for the rest of the group, as well as altering the structure of the drama. On the other hand such casting might be far too difficult for anyone to handle. It is often just as much of a problem to cast the member of the group who insists on taking all the decisions and allows no other authority but his or her own. Such a problem may be tackled as part of the play: 'Does this man speak for all of you?' may be enough, but it may be necessary to stop the play with some pre-arranged signal and sit down and discuss the implications of having so and so in such a position. 'If we are all going to behave like robots who are absolutely under the control of one man, then the play is going to be about that, about absolute power... Is that a change of plan?... Is that what you want the play to be about? ... Shall we go back and try our original idea?' Obviously that is an extreme situation but it is not unknown. The teacher needs to decide whether the power structure within the group is a subject the class should pursue at that moment or whether it is just a matter of mistaken casting, and that by changing her role or the roles of the class, the original play can still advance in some way that is productive and fruitful.

Acquiring necessary skills

There are two main categories of skill needed by any class engaged in classroom drama. One category encompasses all those social skills which make a class easy to work with; the other contains all the communication skills that help the individual to share his understanding of an experience with an audience.

A class that is going to benefit from classroom drama will need a minimum of social skills before it can even begin. These have been referred to earlier, as the minimum requirements for drama. Beyond these lie the further benefits that the individual may acquire by taking part in drama activities.

A teacher faced with a class that cannot tolerate any form of cooperative activity is going to make little headway with drama. Unfortunately there are children like this, who have such problems in relating to other members of the group, that they will not allow themselves to listen to each other, to work together, or even to organize themselves into a space or a circle. Faced with these problems, the teacher has to decide whether to begin drama at all. If she is feeling strong, then she may want to try to gain a measure of cooperation, and it is on such occasions that a more formal approach is usually the only one that seems possible. The children are going to need an imposed structure, since they cannot structure themselves. A great deal depends on their ages, but a possible 'bait' would be working towards some short-term objective (usually performance to others).

The teacher might decide to use video equipment, film or tape as a method of putting together a programme whose content and structure was short, pithy and full of meat. She might decide to use scripted material and concentrate on technique as a way to avoid conflict between individuals. She might want to offer a more individual study of the place of drama in our culture, which included both academic and practical work, such as visiting theatres, looking at historical models, and trying out various actor/audience relationships by doing pieces in the manner of the various periods of theatre history. She might work with the class on acting exercises, beginning with each individual working separately under the teacher's control and gradually progressing to pair work, small group work and so on.

At the top of the secondary range the incentive of an examination course is sometimes used to give an obvious goal to a group's work, but lower down the school a bit of harmless bribery may not come amiss. Many adults still remember being coerced into performance as children and finding the experience more enthralling than they had imagined.

The reasonably well-adjusted group will not need such a rigid structure but will be able to tackle a wide number of *social skills*. For example, they should be able to develop the following abilities:

1   to listen to other members of the group
2   to make concessions
3   to act cooperatively
4   to defend an attitude
5   to accept responsibility for their own decisions
6   to take the role of leader
7   to learn to follow
8   to find an appropriate form of language

9   to project themselves into another person's situation
10   to maintain belief in a fictional situation

Communication skills are those which allow the individual to shape and develop material into a dramatic form as if it were going to be performed, as well as those needed during an actual performance. These were described in the introduction, as the skills of the dramatist and those of the performer. An individual may develop the following skills:

1   to find the climax of a situation
2   to make himself heard clearly
3   to assist in furthering the plot
4   to make belief convincing to others
5   to create character truthfully
6   to sustain concentration
7   to move with assurance
8   to create a piece of group work with artistic integrity

And when using scripted material one may add:

9   the ability to appreciate style
10   to read aloud with conviction

In trying to achieve any one of the preceding skills, the teacher is likely to find, as with every approach to teaching drama, that the first requirement is that she should honestly state her objective to the class. If, for example, she thinks that the time is right for a group to shift emphasis from working with scripts to a rather freer dramatic exploration of the same situation because she feels that they need to gain confidence in using their own words, then she can introduce a new method of working very simply (as in *Lesson 5* on page 71). It is usually true that the more straightforward the approach to the work, the easier it is for everyone. A class needs flexibility and variety of approach and it is too easy to run a series of 'popular' classes without any progression on the part of the group, by falling into a pattern of repeating things that the class finds easy or enjoyable, or by feeling bound to stick to scripted material because the class will not leave the security of the written word.

Neither is it necessary to plan a course that runs from movement and music in the junior school through improvisation exercises to the 'goal' of a written script as the final test. A really productive drama course will include a rich mixture of approaches and should be set out rather differently.

For example, let us say that the teacher has selected as a target or objective for the lesson *the ability to defend an attitude*, because her pupils are disinclined to value their own opinions and usually wait to be told what to think. In this case she may well decide to set up a situation where she can act as devil's advocate, taking a stand that she knows will be unpopular where her arguments will be weak, but strongly held. Whatever situation or context she uses—let us say a group of prisoners—she will allow the class time to establish the reality of the 'as if' of prison life, in whatever way she chooses. She can then offer a fresh turn to the situation by taking the role of an informer or some such character (see *Lesson 3*, page 65), thereby turning the class against her so that all their powers of argument will have to be used, either to persuade her to change, or to decide what punishment should be used (the play can always be stopped, short of the actual carrying out of sentence!). This improvised play may take a whole lesson, allowing time for discussion afterwards; but instead of looking for another 'subject' for the lesson next week, or another activity for the remainder of a longer session, it might be very appropriate for that class to discover what other people have done in the same situation and what words and arguments they have used.

There are many available play scripts, scenes from novels, articles in journals, memoirs and so on which can be used, not to show how it ought to have been done, but how other people's attitudes were either similar or different.

This material can be read by the class if they can read dialogue quickly enough to be effective, or they could listen to a reading of it by the teacher or could watch a video-tape or listen to a recording. A video camera is one of the most useful tools in enabling children to see their own work, providing there is enough light in the room to obtain satisfactory pictures. Some teachers tape-record material (using their friends or other colleagues) to present an idea quickly and easily. Whatever the method chosen, it helps the class to regard drama as something more than a pleasurable activity and it helps the teacher to adopt a more analytical and straightforward approach. The material produced by the children can be viewed as an interesting example of human behaviour and they can then make comparisons with other people's versions.

Sometimes a class will offer suggestions from their own experience and such occasions are to be treasured. They are more likely to occur if the teacher has maintained an appreciative and detached view whilst sharing, as one of the group, in the work in hand.

As an example of the way one might structure a lesson to achieve a skill taken from the second list, let us assume that the teacher wishes the group to tackle number five: *to create character truthfully*.

She could begin by talking her class through a sequence where they reproduce in their own bodies some of the physical effects of extreme old age. This should avoid the cliché of the doddering old fool. She might then come into the situation as the warden of a day centre and set up some activity—getting a cup of tea and sitting down again, making baskets or something similar, all the while encouraging the class to concentrate on the physical representation of elderly people. She can then change gear, as it were, and almost imperceptibly introduce the problem-solving part of the lesson where the characters are led into the situation by having to face a decision about their future. This could be an ultimatum either about moving to another area or about having to enter an old people's residential home, or some such problem. The objective here is to cause them to fill out the background for themselves, to create some life for the people outside the restrictions of the play itself. Therefore, they might be asked to tell the warden why they should not be moved, they might be interviewed by social workers (other members of the class), or they might be asked to write a letter of application for the new home. Whatever the method chosen, the objective is to round out a character. Where a 'role' represents only the attitudes required within that situation, the 'character' is not just a representative of the elderly point of view, he has an individual life style and also begins to look and sound like that particular old person.

This skill of physical personification is not necessary for the conduct of a drama lesson, but it is a necessary part of presenting work to others and therefore is regarded as a performance skill.

Selectivity
One of the skills that a class needs to learn in order to get the most out of shaping its own drama and perhaps showing it to other people, is the ability to be selective.

In their own games children will pursue a topic until they have grown out of it. In a drama lesson this merely becomes tedious unless they can be helped to find new depths in the situation. On the other hand, there is also something to be gained from looking at the dramatic shape of a scene and at how a dramatist selects the most significant moments and does not try to include everything. Drama is not real life and it can be productive to work very occasionally on what to pick out for emphasis and what to eliminate.

One way of doing this is to ask the class, working in groups, to enact short episodes or stories, working to a scenario (such as a synopsis of a TV play or magazine short story or précis of a scene from an actual stage-play). Having presented these fairly rapidly to the rest of the class, thereby enabling them to gain the necessary information, they might then select the theme that they think is central to the scene, the climax of the action, the moments that demonstrated most significantly what the central theme was, or indicated relationships most clearly. They can then either re-enact the scene looking for a way of eliminating everything that is not relevant to those objectives, or try their hand at writing dialogue or create a 'freeze-frame' grouping of the significant moment where the play began and go on from there.

Even if a class is not concerned in performing plays to other people, a short time spent on the art of being selective helps a group to look for the significant moment in all their drama and may help to avoid endless 'playing house' on the part of the younger children.

Whatever the skill she wishes her class to acquire, the teacher should plan her lesson with that as her main objective. She will, of course, find that there are many other skills being used at the same time, but it is the ability to structure a lesson to achieve an objective that is important, rather than trying to find subjects for dramatization. It is not 'making up a play about circuses' that is important; it is using the circus situation to find out more about the group's ability to tackle responsibility or accept leadership, that lies behind the most productive classroom drama.

5

Developing and deepening the drama

Building belief

Since the willing suspension of disbelief is the primary factor in all drama, some attention should be paid to the methods that are available for aiding it. If we accept that the teacher's attitude from the beginning is the most important factor, and that she can establish in the first lesson a safe way of allowing belief to take place and to be built slowly and painlessly, then what more can she provide in future?

The majority of classes must have the need for belief emphasized over and over again.

Many outsiders watching a drama class will say, 'They were all so involved', as a measure of the degree of belief. Often teachers use concentration exercises to develop the ability to focus attention and to foster involvement, whereas it is within the drama itself that attention needs to be paid to the degree of belief that is demanded. In a large group children may opt out for various reasons at different times. Some may never opt in with any depth of feeling. What we are aiming for is a way of building up the individual's commitment to the activity of the rest of the group while the drama is in progress, even if we admit that total absorbtion of the whole group all the time is very rarely achieved.

If the teacher is trying to embark on a single piece of drama which is going to last the group for a whole lesson, there are going to be gradually increasing depths of belief in the 'Big Lie'.

Individual commitment

For example, having started a play about a Roman garrison in Britain (objectives: 1) interdependence within a group, 2) a study of Roman Britain as a project), the teacher felt that it was still very much a game that the children were playing to humour her. They were still 'in the classroom' and the fictional situation was not real for them. So she took the role of a new, young officer sent out from Rome, talking to them as seasoned campaigners who had just fought a serious and deadly battle. She said that her first job on meeting her new command was to find out what the cost had been in men and materials. She asked them to fall in and said that she would inspect their armour. There was a good deal of giggling and acting of a rather facetious nature. The teacher walked up and down the lines of soldiers and whenever a child seemed to be taking things at all seriously she addressed a few words to him or her, using a formal and elevated style of language:

'I see that you have fought bravely. Your armour is only damaged in the front.'
'Soldier, I am pleased that your sword has seen much action.'
'Judging by the damage upon your shield the fighting must have been terrible. You must be a brave warrior.'

The class began to settle down, and their natural competitiveness made them all want to be brave warriors. The teacher walked round to the front and addressed them all: 'Soldiers, will you draw your weapons that I may see that every one of you has taken his toll in the fighting.'

In this way the teacher ensured that each one committed himself to the following ideas:
1   He or she was a soldier.
2   They had fought bravely.
3   They had not had an easy time.
4   The battle was over and the cost had to be counted.
5   They were disciplined troops.

If they could continue to believe in these ideas it would prove easier to move them on to the central theme of the lesson which was that being part of a garrison in a foreign country meant learning to get on with others. By casting herself as a young officer out from Rome, she had authority; but she could afford to drop back and allow the class to make decisions based upon their greater experience of the countryside, as soon as she could see that, as a class, they were capable of taking the drama seriously.

Having ensured a degree of belief in the idea, she then had to push on further. She asked the soldiers to form a circle when dismissed. She dismissed them formally and they sat in a circle on the floor. She asked them to describe for her the worst moment of the battle. She kept the whole atmosphere very formal as if each were giving a report. They stood up and stepped one pace forward into the circle if they wished to speak. The teacher questioned or made some comment upon each report, taking whatever the soldiers said at its face value, even if she had sometimes to adjust the statement a little to avoid glaring anachronisms, which were causing others difficulty in believing. For example, if the whole group had taken mention of cannons as gospel truth, she would have let it go until the end of the play when they could have looked it up, but if one boy said 'cannons' and the others tittered or said, 'They didn't have guns, stupid!' then she would try to keep the class in the context of the play by saying something like, 'Whatever weapons these barbarians have, they are obviously not to be taken lightly,' before passing on to the next man. Demonstrating a firm hold on one's own belief is the best way of deepening that of others.

Ritual
Getting an individual commitment is one way of building belief. Another is to establish some sort of ritual action. There was a ritual element in the Roman play and this can often prove helpful. The classic models for our ideal drama teacher used ritual speech or behaviour as an aid to building belief. Ritual behaviour is obviously appropriate in a play with an historical background. There is immense satisfaction in acting out a knightly vigil or taking an elaborate oath of fealty. In a modern setting the same degree of belief may be achieved by substituting contemporary rituals such as the equipment check and count-down in a spacecraft. Even simple actions such as remembering to open an imaginary door every time someone enters the room or establishing the credentials of every entrant into the Youth Club can serve the same purpose.

Occupational mime
Some preliminary exercises in miming actions with care and precision can form stepping-stones to believing in something like the factory or the kitchen, when a facile waving of the hands will not serve the same end. Children are sometimes embarrassed at their own lack of skill and will make a kind of shorthand gesture where a piece of realistic mime would make all the difference. This does not mean the balletic or the traditional mime. It simply means making believable attempts at working at something imaginary with your hands.

A class who were doing a play about finding the treasure of El Dorado were fooling about at being divers. What was necessary was a piece of teacher-directed movement to practise the actions of a diver under water so that when it was time to come back to that action in the play they could go into it more easily without having to bother about 'how divers signal to each other'. This meant that they could concentrate on the main issues of finding or not finding the treasure, and who were the rightful owners of it.

Even the actions of preparing and serving food during a break in some journey, or the actions of sailors on board ship, or the basket-work of the old people in the home, have a purpose in strengthening reality and are most easily done without the bother of using real objects.

Creating the background
A group may be helped to suspend disbelief by being given some peg to hang the drama on. Some of these 'props' have been mentioned already: photographs of people in the same situation (pioneers or refugees), period

pictures and so on, a rudimentary map on which they can plot their own location, a sacred object which must be protected. There are, however, many things which can be manufactured during the play which can productively aid belief: letters home from the trenches, application forms to be filled in before embarking on some new adventure, 'biographies' to be compiled, petitions, lists of precious objects, census details and so on. There is no reason why a drama lesson should not encourage other ways of working. One class of infants were so convinced that the evil days which had come upon their tribal village were caused by the great eagles hovering overhead, that it became necessary to return to the classroom from the hall and deal with the problem of the eagles. Some made themselves eagle masks and wings that they could wear to lure the birds down. Others made kite-like paper birds to dangle for the same purpose. The remainder of the class either drew or made clay models of the traps that would be needed and the route to the mountain where the eagles had their nests.

It must be admitted that the move to the classroom in this case was also conditioned by the need to set up the dinner tables, but the point is that the fiction was still going on even though the activity had changed.

Subject matter

If, as teachers, we accept that drama is not really a subject but more accurately a process, then we must inevitably come to the conclusion that the content of the lesson is not likely to be the primary concern. The teacher is more likely to ask, 'What experience do I want these young people to have? Do they need to be themselves or someone else? Are they interested in making suppositions about what might happen to them in the future or re-playing their relationships with other people? Are they asking to tackle ideas and concepts which lie far outside their own experience?'

Then comes the stage where she has to ask, 'How do I know what they want?' Asking the class may not work; they may not be able to give a satisfactory answer. Probably if they could, they would already have progressed so far towards an understanding of themselves as a group that the drama they need is the kind that allows them to communicate that understanding to others.

How else can the teacher assess what subject matter to use? The answer must depend on the amount of contact she has with a class and that means not only contact within a drama framework but any kind of contact. For example, what kind of creative writing do they produce? What has really caught on in a history lesson? What are they considering in social studies, religious and moral education or geography? A certain amount of normal staffroom gossip may produce clues that will be useful leaders (without unnecessary 'spying') into issues such as discipline, authority, punishment, self assurance, restlessness, responsibility, and so on.

Another way to assess the pertinence of subject matter is to enquire into the books they enjoy (in or out of class), their other kinds of reading—papers, comics, magazines—and, more importantly, their choice of television programmes. Choice here is vital because the young individual is so often limited by the rest of the family's taste. A few moments spent chatting to a class will often provide at least a way of assessing their general attitudes towards life and their mood on that day. It is sometimes possible to have a range of stimulus material around the room which provides a very clear pointer towards the direction of a class's interests. Suppose, for example, that the teacher puts a screamer headline on the wall and the class read it out in any way that is not dismissive, then that could very well provide the subject of next week's lesson (even this week's if it has been possible to guess the reaction accurately or if planning is not necessary). Newspaper photographs, pictures from magazines, historical material, a skull, a couple of masks, some stage make-up, some mirrors, books, political pamphlets, magazine articles, pictures from films and plays, even junk which they can fiddle with, can all give the observant teacher an idea of the way the young people see themselves and the general area of their interests.

Sometimes teachers conduct a survey, in order to find out those topics that catch their pupils' attention. This can then lead on to stockpiling material that relates fiction to reality. Newspaper articles and photos can be set alongside novels, paintings, poems and song lyrics, to serve as the raw material of future drama lessons.

In ideal circumstances a teacher may be able to work in tandem with another teacher. (There are examples of this in the *Lessons* section.) One example of the way a chosen subject can produce a whole subtext of other themes and issues emerged when a history teacher worked in collaboration with a drama teacher in trying to illuminate some of the issues that led to the English Civil War. The young people involved themselves in the case of Thomas Wentworth, Earl of Strafford. During the working out of the drama the history teacher noted down those issues which would be worth following up in her lessons, while the drama teacher, who was working in role with the class, simply tried to remember anything significant. One girl happened to express a quite serious desire to see an execution. It was quickly passed over in the heat of the moment, but the drama teacher filed it away in her memory for future reference. It was not something that was applicable to further history lessons, but there might be significance in the fact that a fourteen year old girl wanted to watch someone die. It is certainly not the first time such a thought has occurred to a teenager. It is a subject that the adolescent finds of vital interest. If the teacher could make that area of thought accessible, through drama, she might well be helping young people to come to terms with their own feelings. Of course she has a responsibility to the sensibilities of the rest of the class, and it may well be ill-advised to take a chance remark as a basis for a whole lesson; but supposing that chance remark were repeated in some other way, interest in a news photograph for example, then the teacher might well plan a lesson which abstracted that thought and made it available in some form. She could look not only at capital punishment but at that part of human nature that takes pleasure in the pain of others, in our own and other circumstances. She could find a piece of literature, a poem or an extract from a novel. She could take a play such as *Oedipus Rex* or Edward Bond's *Saved* or a piece of sociological material such as an American Indian ritual and use that as the basis for the lesson. The dramatic experience itself had suggested its own follow-up material.

Planning a sequence of lessons

So much depends on beginning a lesson in the right way and setting the emotional temperature at the right level from the start, that continuing the sequence is something which appears relatively easy. There can, however, be some unexpected difficulties. This is particularly true at secondary level. A primary teacher has fewer problems in relating drama to the rest of her work than a secondary teacher who may have to make other, more tenuous links. If drama is seen as an integral part of other classroom work, then English teachers can relate drama to both reading and writing. History or humanities teachers have a wealth of themes to draw on, as have teachers of social studies and other subjects. But the specialist drama teacher who meets a class only once a week may have to ensure that the sequence of lessons follows a logical pattern of its own. She may be able to consult her colleagues on the subject matter and issues that are likely to form part of their lessons, since drama could well provide a useful way of exploring such material, whilst at the same time the learning that has been going on in other lessons can serve to enrich the content of the drama. (There are examples of this sort of two-way traffic in the lessons in *Chapter 6*.) But what is essential is to remember that whereas in the teacher's mind the progress of her pupils may be behavioural or psychological, in their minds there is a need for some obvious pattern of theme or material. In a way every lesson on the secondary timetable requires a fresh start. For the teacher who has a clear scheme worked out, the sight of 3B turning up for drama will probably bring the whole of last week's lesson flooding back into her memory. For the class, however, it is a different matter. A whole week has been spent in other pursuits, following different methods; besides which they have been living at a faster, more intense rate than any adult. For better or worse 3B is a different class this week from what it was last week.

In planning her own sequence of work, what is usually necessary is for the teacher to burrow round in the impressions left after the lesson, and to note down some of the ideas, expressions, antipathies, difficulties and downright blockages that occurred, usually in one word mnemonics, so that they may be sifted out to serve in planning the next lesson. There are examples of this kind of assessment in the sample lessons. The next step is to turn just one of those impressions into a considered subject that does not necessarily reveal the whole of the teacher's motivation, but which will make sense to the class.

It is often possible to ask the class at the end of a session where they think the drama should go next, but it is usually unwise to make a firm promise—too much can happen. An idea hot off the press at the end of a really good lesson can look remarkably shabby at the beginning of the next. It is often more satisfactory to jot down the ideas and say, 'I'll give it some thought and see if I can find a way of looking at that next time.' A class who have had a good experience may want to repeat the idea, on the theory that they can continue to get some buzz from it. The chances of that happening are remarkably slim. It may be that they need to look at the same idea in another way because the idea itself has not been exhausted. They may want to put a gloss on the performance by trying to find out what it was that excited them. The teacher will have to decide, by the form their comments take, which way to go. In any event, she will have to plan a whole new lesson. Repeating the last one never works.

As an example of a simple sequence of short lessons, the teacher could choose as subject matter 'applying for a job'. The reason might be that the young people in her class are not used to working as a whole group, she has a room with furniture in it and there are exams going on in the building so that any activity must be a quiet one. There are several ways of organizing the beginning of such a sequence, but to take just one:

1. The teacher provides the class with an advertisement (real or invented) for a trainee in some appropriate local field of labour. She asks the class to imagine that they are the sort of young person who might apply for such a job and gets them either to write a letter of application or (depending on their ability in writing) to complete an application form which the teacher has made out or obtained. She encourages them to consider an appropriate background for their invented character. She collects the letters.

2. The next lesson follows on. The teacher sets up interviews. If the group is a very small one (often a difficult situation for drama) she can conduct the interviews herself, otherwise she can appoint interviewers, choosing perhaps those whom she can trust or those who do not easily assume another character or who have a delicate sense of self-regard and need to feel safe. At the end of a prescribed time she will need to know how many 'trainees' would be suitable to take on for a trial period, about one third of the group, for example.

3. It is possible that the students have not taken this very seriously. Nevertheless, at this stage some discussion about how the idea can be extended may be useful, to slow down the thinking and to allow the teacher to follow some of the class's ideas.

4. This might include:
  (a) devising tests for aptitude.
  (b) showing the candidates how the job is done, using 'experts' from the rest of the group.
  (c) discussing whether some 'characters' might find difficulty and others might sail through, then demonstrating those situations.

Those elements which the class select as affecting a trainee's success or failure in the job should be jotted down. It could be very productive to have a dossier on the 'trainees' mounted on a piece of paper on the wall, with pictures cut from magazines or drawn by the class, and descriptions done by the interviewers as well as by the candidates themselves. Thus the character 'John Brown' has a school record, a home background, is known to the police, has a girlfriend and so on. By spending time on seemingly undramatic activities, the teacher and the class have stockpiled information for further lessons which can either continue on a quiet classroom level or as an exercise in dramatic biography, resulting in a number of plays about trainees and their relationships with other people at work. It could also develop into a series of other plays taking each character at a time and focusing on what his future (or past) might be, then making comparisons. This could lead to some reading: for example, there are many plays by Barry Keefe, Peter Terson and Bill Owen, among others, that deal with young people at work.

Recently a bill went through parliament which stipulated that schools should inform parents about whether sex education was being taught in order that they might withdraw their children if they felt strongly opposed to it. The following day a radio programme included an interview with a head teacher of a mixed comprehensive school, who when asked who handled sex education in her school said that the drama department did. This occasioned no comment, no surprise. The subject matter of drama is, after all, human relationships. On the whole, though, the drama teacher should retain the right to select the material that is seen to be the most appropriate, or to work closely with other departments, rather than finding herself stuck with a syllabus that stipulates, for example, that in the fourth year of secondary school the drama department is responsible for human biology. Much the most appropriate method is to look for the material that is already in the child's cultural and educational environment and then to explore how drama can serve to illuminate that material.

Developing language

The way language is used and developed in drama is such a large subject that it is impossible to do more than to set out certain signposts so that the teacher may become aware of the potential that exists for herself and for her group.

Working in educational theatre where a programme is repeated many times over, without normally being scripted in any exact way, one becomes increasingly aware of the normal human being's sensitivity to the spoken word. This is naturally true of 'bad' language where people find the words often more offensive than the idea, but it is also significantly true that finding the right tone or pitch of language can make all the difference to the success or failure of a lesson.

If one assumes that anyone who is likely to teach drama in school has at least a nodding acquaintance with the major works of English dramatic literature, then one may also assume that they would be able to use a variety of styles in their own role-play. It is often in the use of an elevated style that one may add a believable tone to a play set in another age. It is by the sensitive choice of vocabulary that the teacher may draw children to find a universal truth within the particular moment of their own creation. It is by the tone of voice that one may suggest either a doom-laden atmosphere or a briskly active and positive approach.

As well as becoming very aware of her own style of language use, the teacher should be able, through drama, to extend her pupils' ability to find an appropriate mode of expression for unfamiliar concepts and situations. Without becoming bogged down in a marsh of theory, it is an obvious truth that, by extending one's ability to put words to thoughts, one is often extending the ability to think. If a teacher can examine the clichés that tend to cut off further thinking, she may well be able to extend her pupils' command of expressive language for the future.

Often the drama moves at such a pitch of excitement that examples of an unusual and extended use of language slip by unrecorded, but if the group are working seriously, the teacher has set the right tone, and the problems facing the group are sufficiently extending (but not beyond their comprehension), then one usually finds that their powers of expression match up to the occasion.

A teacher should not be afraid of adopting a more formal style of language herself when working with children. It is no more than using a 'bookish' style when reading, and it does help to establish that this is not a normal situation, that the normal rules do not apply, and that therefore the normal forms of expression are not enough. A group of miners will not use the same forms of expression as a group of Red Indians and it is important that the language of both groups should be essentially different from that used in the classroom—not in pronunciation, but in imagery and vocabulary and in the concepts that are being handled.

This often means that things proceed more slowly, because time must be given to finding the most appropriate form of expression, not only for the occasion, but to suit the subject. For example, finding the best way of conveying to the angry king that an expedition to Guyana would 'bring him benefits untold to man', whilst at the same time persuading him that Sir Walter Raleigh had 'served his sentence and done his time', would not necessarily be the historically appropriate phrases you would find in a book, but they are exactly right for the children's purposes.

It is also true that a teacher and class while working in role, may use highly provocative and even abusive language to good effect, without losing face. Should the child of twelve be penalized, who at the height of a period of frustration and anger at his authority being challenged turned to the teacher and said, 'Look you, why don't you piss off and leave us alone to manage our own affairs?'

It may be just as shocking to the class when their teacher becomes helpless, miserably weak and whining. 'I don't know how to do it,' she moans; 'You'll have to do it for me.' Will they be able to cope with the responsibility of handling such an unpleasant and dependent creature who has reversed her normal caring and authoritative role? Will they find it merely funny or unduly irritating?

The way that a teacher asks questions is also something that needs careful thought. Can the teacher frame questions in such a way that the class is led forward in its search for an answer? Can the teacher reflect or muse aloud in such a way that the class is allowed to glimpse a universal truth beyond their actions? Can she question in a way that challenges limited responses and can she elicit information and cause a class to be analytical about its work? Sometimes when planning a lesson, it is productive to list some of the questions one might find useful in that situation, even though they may never be used: so that if a play seems to be heading in one direction or another, one is not caught out.

For example, if a group of children who are not usually very profound thinkers are doing a play where they are leading a stranger through a subterranean passage, the plot could easily become a series of adventures, each one happily surmounted—sharks, falling rocks, vampire bats and other 'James Bond' situations. How can the teacher (the stranger) frame questions to deepen the thinking without spoiling the fun? The children are not going to want to stop inventing horrors and would only become very frustrated if the stranger refused to go any further, but these children are getting nothing from the play other than pleasurable fear, coupled with the ease with which they prove that they can surmount every difficulty. The teacher has to think very quickly and decide how she can proceed.

In one such lesson (involving an E.S.N. class), the best way seemed to be to use the fear itself versus the ease of overcoming it as a central factor, so the teacher called a halt for a rest, purporting to be unable to go forward and asking for a safe place to be found. The children found a suitable ledge and produced some unexplained food, which was not questioned, and the teacher said, 'Do you know, I'm beginning to wonder about something. Something very strange.' There was a pause while the children's attention was caught, then she said, 'Do you think by any chance, that all these frightening things are not real after all?' One girl immediately 'saw' another bat to prove that they still existed. Quickly the teacher intervened, to prevent a repetition of the pretended terror, and said, 'I'm wondering whether things like that are a sort of test ... if perhaps they only exist *because* we're frightened. Perhaps that's what happens when people find themselves alone in dark caves and passages. Perhaps they imagine horrid things and make themselves frightened. Should we try going on, very quietly, without being afraid and see if I'm right?' The children quickly agreed without thinking very much and one boy suggested singing, which they did. The teacher proposed that just one of them, someone who felt very brave, should go ahead, and this idea was quickly accepted so that the remainder of the class could discuss the effect on the 'bats' before leaving that subject. They could say, 'Yes, it was true, there wasn't really anything there; it was only being frightened that made the sharks and bats come out.' (They did not cease to exist, they only did not *come out!*) After that the play changed direction and the teacher was able to bring it back to its original setting and round it off, with the class telling the whole story to a 'policeman' as a way of summarizing it.

What is interesting in this example is not the outcome or subject matter of the play, but the teacher's attempt to use words to give an implication to the children's playing of 'spooky' games, and to turn the play into something that had universal application—people invent things to be afraid of, in order to explain why they are afraid!

There is no certainty that the children in that special school will remember anything of that lesson, and if they do, it will probably be the enjoyment of pretending to be frightened, but if part of the purpose of drama is to extend language and to extend fictional experience beyond playing games, then for a moment at least that lesson had something in common with *Pilgrim's Progress*. By using a reflective kind of language to dress up the incident they had created the same function for their drama as the little girl who invented the Big Bad Wolf in the lavatory. It is often the responsibility of the teacher to introduce that kind of universality by the use of appropriate language, because in so doing she can force the drama into a wider context.

Because drama provides a fictional framework for the use of language it is often noticeable that children will be forced to struggle with concepts and emotions that they do not usually have to put into words. More important still is the fact that in a dramatic situation people *listen*.

So often a child finds himself unheard because what he is saying is unimportant or irrelevant to the people who surround him. This is not necessarily because they are unkind or indifferent. It may be that there is no coincidence between their view and the child's view of the same situation. In drama, there is a greater degree of congruity. This is particularly true if the teacher helps the class to focus their attention on a central, important issue and then allows them to think about it. In this way whatever a child says becomes important and the moment can be extended to allow everyone whatever time is needed to tackle that issue.

The following extracts from a transcript of a tape-recording show the efforts made by a group of young people to struggle with unfamiliar concepts, and to try to find a style and vocabulary to communicate with each other and with the teacher.

The teacher had taken the role of Margaret Guizer, a fictional character who exemplified the early Quakers. This was suggested by the lesson on war (*Lesson 3*). She had wanted to examine the degree to which it is possible to commit oneself to an opinion, to follow a strongly held lead, and at what point an opinion can become a dangerous obsession. The class had been strongly motivated to commit themselves to a set of rules. The majority had been allied with Margaret and had said they would be willing to try to become totally non-violent whatever the provocation. The minority worked with another teacher who gave another set of rules, those of total conformity with law and order, as 'Guardians' of the Tower of London.

The 'Guardians' arrested the 'Friends' and asked them to swear an oath of allegiance. Some children opted out of the problem, modified their belief and took the oath. Their responsibility then became one of persuading both extremes, from their middle standpoint, to take a more reasonable attitude. There was then a long period of negotiation. The outsiders (called *O.* in the transcript) tried to persuade the prisoners (*P.* in the transcript) to sign and be released. They also acted as negotiators with the Guardians (*G.*). (The teacher is *M.*)

Religious belief is a tricky subject in many multi-racial schools. How does the individual child face a matter of conscience? Many of the others had made up their minds. One quiet boy, David, was still wrestling with the problem and could not decide where to place his allegiance.

D. Friend Margaret?
M. Yes.
D. What must I do? You see I'm a Catholic, but I believe what you say ... about not fighting.

> **M.** Are you not sure about taking the oath?
> **D.** I want to be with you.
> **M.** If you are worried ... what does your conscience tell you to do?
> **D.** I don't think I am loyal to the King ... I don't agree with the King.
> **M.** Do you have to agree? Can you ... in friendship ... just listen to what he says?
> **D.** But I don't have to swear to him?
> **M.** Not if you don't think it's right.
> **D.** Then I'll come with you.

Without making too much out of such a short piece, what seems immediately important is the fact that David was bringing his *real* situation (his Catholicism) into a fiction (non-conformity and the King) and looking to a fictional character (Margaret) for a lead. The role served two purposes for him, teacher and agitator. By answering mainly with another question, Margaret refused to tell him what to think, but offered the security ('I want to be with you.') of reassurance in the statement, 'Not if you don't think it's right.' The central issue had ruffled David's security and he was having to consider the concept of loyalty. Normally he would go along with the majority of his mates. The teacher knows that he is going to find no security in siding with her.

In the 'dungeon' the prisoners immediately create an appropriate atmosphere. (It was a dark area but it was warm and dry.) They used words to convey the 'feel' they wanted.

> **P.1** It's cold down here.
> **M.** It may get worse.
> **P.1** Will we be executed?
> **M.** I don't know.
> **P.2** I doubt it.
> **P.3** They said persuade us.
> **P.4** Torture!
> **P.2** Oh! Sh!
> **P.4** They might torture us.
> **P.3** They might separate us and torture us and see if that would change our minds.

In this example the children are using words to build up a sensation which they feel is necessary to convince themselves of the reality of the dungeon.

During negotiation the prisoners found it easier to use a more formal and elevated style of language than either the Guardians or the Outsiders. They had already established their own belief. The Outsiders tried to maintain their own language levels at first, as one child to another.

O. Come out. Swear the Oath.

P. Never.

O. You've got to.

P. Never. I'll never be made to swear.

O. Why not?

P. I don't take orders from anyone. Only from God.

O. Look, anyone could get through these bars. Easy.

P. We're here of our own free will. They're trying to get us to escape. Look, we could come out at any time. We could walk out of here if we wanted. We *choose* to be here.

It was at this point that the Outsiders needed to reconsider the way they were approaching the Prisoners. They began to expand their arguments and incidentally used a more elevated style of language.

O. Come out. Swear the Oath.
You want to be friends with everyone. *Everyone.* Not just that. . . (indicating Margaret).
They say you can go free. Be free. Just sign. Don't you want freedom? How can you be Friends or *show* you are Friends if you are in prison? If you are *dead?*
God doesn't forbid you to sign. You're not disobeying God.

Again, in the above extract, the question of loyalty is paramount. The argument is about a straight choice between friendship in the normal sense of the word and the extreme attitude taken by the prisoners.

The Guardians take another stance. Their language use varies between the shouting, bullying tone they imagine a jailor would use and a more persuasive, argumentative level which their task imposes on them.

P. Stop trying to persuade us. We're not going to change our minds.

G. Then you'll just rot. Come on. Why not get it over with? It's better than sitting down here.

P. Anything's better than sitting down here. Of course it is.

G. Then why don't you sign? Sign!
All you have to do to prove your loyalty is just sign. It's stupid. Put your name on a piece of paper.

At this point an order was shouted outside the dungeon and the Guardians made a move to obey.

P. So. You can only act because of the laws.

G. You can have friends, you can move around. You can see your friends.

P. (Taking advantage of a seeming ascendancy over the Guardians who now seem to be prisoners of their own law.) You get ordered around!

G.1 *You* won't get ordered around.

G.2 If there was no order around here what would it be like? I mean a criminal could just walk on the street.

G.3 I see! So you'd just say 'Hullo, Friend' and get killed.

G.4 We won't kill you. All you have to do is just sign and you're free to go. It's better than sitting down here.

G.5 It's also better than being killed just so's you can go around saying ... Hullo Friend, what's your name? ...

The last speaker may have created an absurd muddle between being dead and walking around but in the event nobody noticed the absurdity and on the superb panache of a dramatic statement about dying for one's principles, the Guardians swept out. They had raised the level of the language they were using from repeating 'Swear the Oath', to a style of heightened dramatic prose in longer sentences that was both forceful and persuasive. In fact all the children had become dramatists as well as actors; they had modified their style to suit the situation and the characters they were representing.

This is what normally happens in improvised drama of any quality, where there is enough belief in the situation to allow the participants to extend their range of expression beyond the norm and to tangle with concepts that they do not usually have to articulate. The examples given are not unusual or exceptional in any way. The written work which followed was perhaps, if anything, more expressive, being emotion recollected in tranquillity. It is not, however, its unusual quality that is the reason for including it; it is just because it is a very usual thing for children to write vividly as a result of being involved in a piece of drama. If more teachers were aware of drama as a powerful method of helping children to express not themselves so much as universal thoughts and shared concepts, there would not be such a common feeling that drama is a frill that must be put aside when more 'serious' subjects have to be considered. This is also an overwhelming reason for including written work, research, discussion, reading and other art forms as part of the drama curriculum, in order to give a more permanent form to the work, so that it can be remembered and referred to more easily, by becoming objectified.

A Guardian writes his report

There are dangerous people who say that everyone is born equal. It is stupid nonsense. They say you can call a teacher 'friend' and the king by his first name. There is a woman, Guizer, who says this. We threw her down the stairs and she screamed. How could everyone just run about all over the place saying, 'I am your friend' and loving everyone and refusing to fight or do what they are told? They must be mad. We have to show them who is boss. They sat down quick enough when the sergeant shouted at them ... but they won't sign. We can't let them go free because of all the other troublemakers outside. My Lord says, 'put them to be transported'. If they can make a place in America where everyone is equal ... well, good luck. Maybe we do have to take orders, but we can shout at them though, and push them around.

Poems from the dungeons

1.
I am a prisoner in the cell.
Cold, dark cell.
No one to talk to.
Alone with nothing to eat.
Rats scurrying about my feet.
A narrow slit for a window.
When will I be led out to die?
Water drips steadily from the walls.
I see names scratched on the brickwork.
These people never got out.

2.
Go away.
Go away and give me some peace,
Leave me alone,
My life is my own,
I won't swear,
I don't care,
I'll rot down here,
Just stop shouting at me and let me make up my own mind.
'Just say the King is your master,
Only promise to protect him from traitors.'
Traitors! they said *we* were traitors!
Must I betray my friends?
'Swear,
Swear the oath,
Swear.
Why don't you?'
If only I could,
It would be so easy,
Just sign my soul away,
Then walk out
Up the steps
Away from the water that creeps up from the river.
It would be so easy.

6

Lessons

The lessons in this section are examples of one teacher's work. Their only value is in the detailed analysis of one person's planning, approach and results with a variety of classes. They are a way of illustrating some of the methods described in the earlier part of this book and should serve instead of pictures or diagrams. In no way should they be taken as a rule of thumb, but may serve as a reference point for teachers wishing to plan their own lessons along the lines suggested earlier.

There are certain factors which are common to all these lessons and which should, perhaps, be explained. In most cases the lesson involved a whole class working together, with the teacher in role for at least part of the time. This is a personal choice, based on the objectives for this kind of classroom drama. Other methods of teaching would suit other objectives and other subject matter just as well.

The second factor to take into account is that, because the drama involves everyone in the room, the context for the plays often seems similar. Almost all the plays seem to involve tribes, villages, or events from the past. This is because they are concerned with situations which involve anything up to forty people at a time and call for collective decisions. It is therefore only too obvious that these people have to have something that binds them together. They require some common interest—a job, a fellowship, a place, a shared faculty, a need. The historical bias is one of personal taste and interest. There is, however, another claim to be made for using a historical setting for drama. Asking a class to work in a setting far removed in time, place or circumstance from their own often achieves a wider, more universal sense of belonging to mankind. There is a deep satisfaction in finding that people are remarkably the same, whenever and wherever they live.

The third factor is perhaps the most important. In every example the class and the teacher were relatively new to each other. The lessons were given as a form of demonstration in order that the class teacher might observe the children working with someone else. This may, perhaps, be seen as an advantage, since it should be relatively easy to identify the various devices used to fulfil particular objectives with each class. The disadvantage is that the objectives may not be the same as if the teacher and class were meeting on a more permanent basis.

Lesson 1: The cavalry—infants

Objectives To get rid of two commonly held beliefs: that the only appropriate material for very young children is fantasy and that they cannot concentrate for more than a few minutes.

Planning
The class were asked what they wanted to do a play about. The word 'cavalry' was put forward. The teacher was not sure that the children really meant what she understood by cavalry, but on being asked whether they wanted to do a play about soldiers who rode horses, they agreed. The teacher asked if they would allow her to be the Captain, which was also agreed, and they lined up by the door of the classroom ready to go to the hall to 'find their horses'.

During the walk from the classroom to the hall the teacher was planning the lesson.

1   The class was very cooperative and willing to join in, but a bit excitable. Structure and control were going to need to be firm.
2   Some of them did not speak much English, so there would have to be a large proportion of physical activity which must not preclude thinking.
3   Since horses were going to be important, they had to be made very believable, and yet 'riding' round making whinnying noises could be rather unproductive. She decided against riding. The horses were going to be led. What circumstances would enable 'led' horses to constitute a problem? She decided to postpone a decision on that point and concentrate on making the leading of horses the first part of the play.

Outside the door of the hall the 'soldiers' stopped and waited. The Captain said, 'Cavalrymen: When we go in there, I want each man to stand beside his horse, loosen his reins and hold him ready. Now, follow me.' This was said quietly, not barked as an order to soldiers. The Captain stood in the same relationship to the soldiers as a teacher would to a class.

Stage One
The teacher took the children through the stages of building their belief in their mounts, by suggesting that they rub down, check over and feed their horses, accompanying every suggestion with action 'as if' she also held the reins of a large horse. There was a lot of quiet chatter and the class seemed happily busy.

Stage Two

The teacher as Captain tied her horse to a tree and asked the cavalrymen to tether their own horses and sit down. She then asked some of the children questions about their horses—their names, condition, harness, and so on: anxious questions such as, 'You are sure your horse is in good condition?', 'Are his feet sore?', 'Can you manage to keep him warm out of doors at night?'. Some of the children led their horses one by one for the Captain to see. They lifted their hooves and saddles were tested. It became apparent that things were not as good as had first appeared. Many of the imaginary steeds were tired and there was not enough good saddlery or harness, also food was short. The suggestion of being out of doors away from security was enough to produce a feeling that things were in a potentially dangerous state; also, there was a sense that these horses were important—almost loved—by the children.

Stage Three

It was time to introduce the 'problem' part of the drama. Belief was strong, but interest could not be held for much longer. The Captain again took the lead and introduced the next part of the plot. By questioning the soldiers as to whether they had seen anyone hiding in the rocks and hills, a strong atmosphere of danger was built up. Voices were hushed. It looked like an ambush. Somehow they were going to have to get the horses out unharmed.

The teacher realized that the children might want to play soldiers in the sense of 'bang, bang, you're dead', which would spoil the quiet concentration on the reality of their status as 'people who cared for horses'. Not wanting to lose that atmosphere meant that battle must be avoided, so the Captain suggested that they saved the few bullets they had and tried to get away without the enemy seeing them. How could they lead the horses without making a sound? There were so many rocks and stones.

A girl suggested tying rags round each horse's hooves. Did they have rags? A quick discussion led to the decision to cut up blankets. The horses' hooves were muffled. A long procession of silent cavalrymen led their mounts down the gully. To avoid any danger of the enemy coming after them, a huge dam of stones was built to block the stream and create an impassable lake. They crept silently back to the classroom.

Stage Four

The teacher began a story. 'Once upon a time, twenty eight soldiers of the Fourth Cavalry Regiment ...' The children looked round at each other. There *were* twenty eight of them. The story recounted *their* adventures. The danger element was heavily underlined. Every detail of their actions was included. The story ended, 'And to this day the lake that was formed high in the mountains is called The Silent Pool.'

Conclusion

By telling the story back to the children their drama was given a recognizable form. It became satisfactory, and yet it had been a very minor episode. There had been no great drama. No issues of any magnitude had been raised. The two original targets had been reached, however: in the first place, the lesson was not a fantasy lesson, no magic solutions had been used, and secondly, the children's attention had been held by a fictional situation for half an hour (not counting the story). The children who did not speak much English had been involved in the pantomimic element of the play and had understood enough to participate in the action even if they had not fully appreciated the story at the end. Important points to note are the following:

1   This was a one-off lesson. There was no theme or outside teaching element in it.
2   It was concerned with building belief.
3   There was a large element of mimed activity.
4   The teacher kept control in her own hands.
5   Importance was given to the whole by the story-telling.
6   The class worked as individuals within a large group.
7   They were a well-motivated and imaginative group and there were no problems in getting their commitment, so it was possible for the teacher to use their own ideas. Her problem was to give form to those ideas so that they might get the maximum satisfaction.

Future work

Further lessons were not scheduled, but the next element that suggests itself is the placing of some larger problem for the group to tackle. Suppose, for example, some of the horses had had to be killed? Would they have been able to reconcile their feeling for their animals with the safety of the troop?

Such work would be difficult until the command of language amongst this racially mixed group was improved, but drama could offer a way of tackling this problem if the teacher could plan the scale of approach carefully and build on what had already been achieved.

Lesson 2: The tribe—4th year juniors

Objectives The class had been working on a project called 'The Family of Man' and had already studied this particular tribe in considerable detail with another teacher (who had requested the lesson as a way of using drama to enrich the project work). Initially there appeared to be some danger in a dramatic approach, since the tribe's chief concern was fighting, but there was an underlying, implied interest in Western culture and its effect on other people. Because this second idea appealed to the drama teacher, she planned to work in the role of a government agent, who was offering the young people of the tribe the chance to move to the city where they would be given an education.

Stage One
The teacher discussed with the class how they should set up the play. They decided that the government agent should be brought into a tribal assembly by a group of scouts. She then waited on the sidelines while a small group of boys, as self-appointed scouts, organized the rest of the class into the 'assembly'. There was a significant swagger about them which should have given the teacher a warning sign as to what was to follow.

Stage Two
As the government agent the teacher was brought into the assembly, and a good tribal discussion followed, about the relative merits of town and country life. Not everyone spoke but the whole class seemed interested and listened well. The boys took the lead. The major issue was introduced quite quickly, which was that whereas Western education teaches that killing individuals is wrong, these people lived in order to fight and kill. The agent emphasized that even without going to the town, new laws would forbid fighting, and murder would be punished by imprisonment for life. It was at this moment that the lesson changed direction completely.

Stage Three
The dominant group of boys withdrew to make 'secret plans' taking the other boys in the class with them. This left the girls without any motivation. The teacher had to decide whether to stop the play, to try to bring the boys and girls together again or to allow this new development to continue. It was alarming not to know what the boys were planning to do. They had, however, been very constructive in the earlier part of the lesson, so she decided to ally herself with the girls and, if necessary, continue with two groups working simultaneously. The lesson now had a different bias. Was this what the class really wanted to learn? It looked as though what might prove of lasting importance was the relative status of the male and female roles *in the class*. As often happens, the drama of their own situation was more absorbing than the drama introduced by the teacher. Without abandoning the original scheme, could this new learning area be explored? Was there a way in which the teacher could advance the position of these rather submissive girls?

Stage Four
The teacher, still in role, announced that while the men were conferring,

the women would hold a meeting of their own to which the men were not invited. The girls were told that these powerful men would lose all authority if fighting were to be banned by law. In future it would be the things that women had traditionally undertaken that would be important—farming, providing goods for sale in the markets, building houses and rearing families. She asked how they would take over the future running of the tribe. The idea was appealing and produced some excitement. At this moment they were interrupted by the return of the men. They were led by one of the boys, who drew a knife and threatened the teacher with it. There were gasps and much nervous giggling amongst the children and most of them forgot that they were acting. Here was a crisis point, where the teacher had to choose between ending the play or trying to continue. The boy *had threatened the government agent* so therefore she could maintain the drama for at least a moment or two longer. The situation was apt—the authority of the armed man. Also, she felt a degree of personal challenge and was reluctant to concede defeat, so she decided to go on.

Stage Five
She asked the men to listen while the consequences of their actions were explained to them. She used the same vocal tone and manner as she had used throughout to represent the government agent. The boy holding the knife continued to brandish it, but they agreed to listen. It became apparent that this lad was in a vulnerable position as class leader. He needed to save face without having to resort to violence, so the teacher referred to him as 'the Chief Warrior, the Fighting Man', and explained what would happen if a government agent was killed. The final end of the warrior as a powerful factor in the tribe would come about even sooner, in a government prison. She summarized the discussion she had had with the girls, who did not, however, join in and were obviously shocked and intrigued by this new sub-plot of the boy with the knife. The boys were equally shocked by the idea of the girls running the tribe, and they began to shout and bluster. The teacher dropped her role and sat down to discuss the play with the class.

Conclusion
The lesson was not successful in that it did not provide any firm outcome and the final discussion did not produce any great depth of thinking. The teacher side-stepped the issue of the knife being produced in school, deciding to talk privately to the boy on that matter. She found herself in a delicate position because in the first place it was a 'prop' in a play, secondly she was not the class's regular teacher, and finally, although the boy needed to be reminded of the dangers of possessing a knife, it should not be at that moment, when he was still held in some awe by the others.

For the purposes of this book, a full description of this somewhat unusual lesson serves to bring out several points:

1   Very often what the class needs to learn only appears during the course of the play.
2   An intelligent and lively class can often change the focus of a lesson. The teacher has to consider how far they should be encouraged to do so.
3   Because so many issues in the play had nothing overtly to do with the subject matter, there was no final outcome. It seems as though nothing was achieved. There was, however, a great deal of potential for future lessons, especially in raising the status of the girls.

Future work

In a further lesson with this class the teacher might well follow up some of the issues that were raised, by beginning with a game or exercise, using a larger space with the children working in pairs: one as the master and the other as a robot or android. The android only responds to specific orders to move its joints in certain ways: 'Bend your left knee and bring it up in front. Straighten your left leg. Put it down. Bring your head and body over the left leg. Now bend your right knee.' This might be enough to make the android walk. The master tries to get the android to complete a simple task without explaining what the task is. Following this game, the girls would be asked to take up their former roles of the women in the tribe and to try to teach the boys the movements that would achieve a task, without explaining what that task might be. Without losing dignity the boys might be expected to learn the movements and guess the nature of the job. The teacher, assuming the role of an elder of the tribe, would then call an assembly to decide what tasks might be essential for their future welfare. The women, who had previously undertaken all responsibility for these tasks, would now have to organize four or five working groups where the men of the tribe would learn the work from them. Only a few minutes would be spent on this activity, then the elder would call the assembly together again to point out that since there would be no future for any warlike skills, the men would have to learn all the other tribal skills from the women. It would be only right that (being deliberately provocative), the women should govern the tribe in future. The men should no longer make decisions.

There is no saying how this lesson would progress. It is possible that a third lesson would follow, about the qualities needed for leadership. It might be that such issues were better talked about outside the drama lesson. Whatever the outcome, the teacher would certainly want to raise the vital question, 'Who has the ultimate power? The man with the knife?'

Lesson 3: Life in the trenches—4th year juniors

Objectives   To satisfy the need for instant satisfaction in a class which had been fired by the dramatic potential of trench warfare. They had been to a war museum and this had been fruitful material for much research and written work.

Planning
The teacher planned an approach which she felt would help to answer the following questions: Why were these children so fascinated by this subject? Did they glorify war? Had it been glamorized for them?

She planned to work in role but left the defining of her role to the group. She wanted to be able to inject a contrasting mode of thought after the play had begun so she made a theatrical 'prop' which looked like, and sounded like, a morse transmitter. It had a buzzer key similar to a bell-push which was operated by a battery. There were various ways the class might react to this. She kept it in her bag until the time came to use it. The class and the teacher had worked together twice before and a good relationship existed between them.

Stage One
A discussion took place. The teacher reminded the class of the way they had worked in previous lessons when one of the plays they had done had been about a secret hide-out. On that occasion the lesson had been brought to an abrupt halt by some over-enthusiastic work on the part of some of the class. They had introduced a sub-plot which had forced a radically different situation on the others. It was decided that in this lesson the class would try to restrict its activities, by doing a play in which people could not move about freely. The subject of trench life was discussed and the class brought up the difficulty of parts for girls. The teacher saw no reason why all the class should not be soldiers but the girls themselves said they would rather run the supply depot and first aid post. The teacher said that she would start the play off by being an officer, but that she would later take another role.

Stage Two
The school is an open-plan building which has drawbacks for drama. The hall, however, is suitable for drama and has blocks built up as a stage. The teacher made a false start, by beginning the play without realizing that the children would bury themselves behind the blocks. She stopped at once and suggested that they set up the trenches further out in the room because there was a danger of people falling over each other and getting really hurt. She then began the play again, by addressing the class rather abruptly: 'Who's in charge here?' The class indicated the boy who had introduced the counter-plot in the previous play. The

teacher asked about what had happened to their commanding officer, which led to an exchange with the class about a bombardment which had caused considerable casualties. The teacher asked to be taken on a tour of inspection, while the troop settled themselves in for a night in the trenches. This enabled a check to be made on the considerable background information the class had acquired and which they were using to good effect, even though the lesson had barely begun. The class was purposeful and seemed to need little help. The teacher as the officer warned against provoking attacks until they had received reinforcements (to allow time for the play to develop), and told them to 'carry on'.

Stage Three
The teacher stood aside, watching for the moment when she sensed that the class would be ready to move into a different phase in the drama. There was no lack of belief, the class had settled in remarkably quietly. All that was necessary was to try to focus all this wide variety of business so that it became structurally and artistically formulated into 'a play'. She waited until one boy whispered 'Sh! I can hear something', and some of the others crawled over to him. She then sat down on the floor with the buzzer and began to tap out a 'morse' signal.

Stage Four
Her intention was to provide a unifying force to bring the children together, and then to introduce an element of doubt about the rights and wrongs of warfare. She thought they might treat her as a spy, in which case she could plead the case for the enemy. As it turned out, the class accepted her cover story (perhaps because of the initial warning about changing the situation). She said she was a peasant woman, who had lived in the farmhouse they had shelled, whose only reason for sending messages was to pass on information to other people. These facts were grudgingly elicited from this frightened woman after much questioning. When her cover story was accepted, the role was modified to fit, and became more accusing. 'What do you think you are here for? Shelling and burning my house?' 'Protecting you from the enemy.' 'What difference is it to me who burns my house: you, or them over there?' and so on, trying to raise the moral issues of the situation.

Stage Five
Although this section had provided a central focus for the play and had produced some really thoughtful responses from the children, it had not become the dynamic feature it might have been been with a less clearly motivated class. These soldiers still wanted a battle. This time it was they who were not going to be sidetracked. The teacher saw that it would be unreasonable to try and hold back the action any longer. They had not disregarded the moral issues, but they had determined to do a play in which they could fight. In role as the peasant she summed up angrily,

'You see, it doesn't matter what people like me say. We can't stop the killing, we can't stop the burning and the destruction. Go on then, if that's what you want. Fight your filthy war.'

Stage Six
The class acted out a battle in which they blew up an enemy tank, and fired endless rounds into the enemy trenches. Several soldiers were realistically wounded and treated at the first aid post. It was all over in a few minutes, as such plays normally are (which is one reason why one tries not to include battles in classroom drama).

Stage Seven
The class sat down with the teacher, who asked them to write a letter home about the events of that day. This was done instead of discussion for two reasons: time was short and the children were still very excited, therefore writing would serve to give a quiet ending to the lesson; secondly, it would give the teacher some inkling as to whether they attached any importance to the ideas put forward in the middle of the drama.

Conclusion
There are many occasions when a class needs instant satisfaction from a drama lesson. In the event, the battle which the teacher had feared to embark on was conducted in a disciplined way by the class. It is hard to tell whether this was in any way due to the slowing down of the events leading to the battle. The whole lesson lasted an hour and twenty minutes, of which the battle itself took up less than ten. The deeper implications of the situation were understood and expressed in the written work. They were not, however, given any undue importance. Understanding had not led to either acceptance or rejection. They were simply recorded and set aside.

Future work
The teacher had to think about whether the issues were too high-flown for the class to work on, whether she had simply introduced a role with a point of view and not a 'problem', and finally, whether to proceed.

As it turned out, the teacher's own conviction that these issues were too important to be ignored, but that the class had got what they needed at the time and were not ready to go further, led to the development of another sequence of lessons. This time the approach was different. Instead of confronting the class with an opposing point of view, they were given the opportunity of allying themselves to someone who held strong pacifist principles. They could thus test their own ability to carry out a policy of non-violence against extreme provocation. This is the lesson that produced the tapes in the section on developing language.

Lesson 4: The fugitive—lower juniors

Objective In inner city schools it often happens that at the beginning of
the academic year a proportion of children join the class speaking little
or no English. The teacher may also be new to the class and may want to
introduce them to a new way of working and to various styles of drama.

Planning
This lesson involved two teachers who planned and operated what became an educational theatre programme.

The central device used in this lesson is a favourite amongst 'Theatre
in Education' companies, that is, to provide the class with a character
who is completely dependent upon the children. Although this programme was taken to several schools it could have been operated as a
'one-off' lesson using two teachers or a teacher and a student on teaching
practice. There was a tight structure and timing which were pre-determined.

Stage One
The teacher encouraged the children to talk briefly to her about the
subject matter of the play, as well as the title, *The fugitive*, meaning
'someone on the run', with all the concomitant implications of crossing
borders and being unable to return to one's home. The talk also led to
some children describing the process of going through customs. They
were encouraged to demonstrate search methods and the machinery used
at points of entry. Immigration was mentioned and the idea that there
might well be prohibited objects such as bombs, weapons, currency and
drugs, or prohibited *people* such as terrorists, criminals, smugglers and so
on.

This preliminary talk enabled the teacher to assess the language ability, the background knowledge and the degree of involvement in the
subject. It also allowed a certain vocabulary to be introduced and, if
necessary, translated by the other children.

Stage Two
The teacher introduced the idea of doing a play. She suggested that the
class should be immigration and customs officials who would examine
anyone passing through the docks. She took the role of training officer
and explained that although she could be referred to at all times for help
and advice, all decisions would be theirs. She suggested a trial run.

To get some activity going she announced that she would go out and
return, pretending to be a passenger. This would test the way they
examined people coming into the country. She picked up a shoulder bag
with some specially prepared 'props' in it, including an out-of-date
passport and a sweet tin with some harmless tablets (not sweets) in it. On
re-entering the room she took care to look frightened and not to speak

first. The class also looked nervous and giggled, unsure of what to do. Eventually her bag was searched and she was examined and questioned. There was an added thrill in going through an adult's bag, as well as some diffidence about touching the teacher herself.

After a few moments the teacher came out of her secondary role as a passenger and reverted to being a training officer. She commented on the trainees' skill, repeating the phrase 'as immigration officers you will have noticed ...' as often as possible to reinforce their own roles in the drama. She also drew their attention to things they may have missed in her bag and asked whether they would admit such a person to the country.

Stage Three
The beginning of the real drama. The training officer announced that there had been a shooting incident on dock number three in which a sailor from a foreign ship had been killed. She showed them a plastic bag and asked them to examine it and to report on its significance. The bag had in it a large quantity of Greek play-money in notes and coins, a wallet with photographs of people and an imposing building, a jewel box with a 'medal' and a brass eagle, some foreign chocolate wrappers and a couple of Greek stamps. The bag itself was also Greek. The reason for the preponderance of Greek objects was to introduce a different style of lettering and therefore to exclude obvious conclusions. The officers examined the objects and handled them with extreme care. They made their reports. Suddenly the quiet was interrupted by the door being thrown open and a figure stumbling into the room. The man fell to the ground exhausted. His trousers were torn at the knee. He was bleeding. He had a gun in his nervous fingers. He was breathing in gasps and was terrified.

This moment of high theatricality shocked the children by its sheer surprise. They did not know whether to giggle, shriek, run, jump into action, or how to behave! They knew that it was a play but they had been surprised into a new kind of activity. They recognized stage blood and a toy gun, but they wanted above all to go along with the potential they saw in the fiction.

Stage Four
Remembering that this was a lesson to encourage those with a limited grasp of English, the fugitive made no recognizable sound and reacted strongly to being crowded. He made enormous efforts to understand and reply in odd English words, when quiet attempts at communication were made. The teacher had a large number of paper handkerchiefs in her bag and these were used to bandage the wounded knee. He had identity papers.

The whole of this section of the lesson was occupied by the attempts of the children to find a common language of signs, drawing, single words, any unusual languages—Hindi or Polish, *any* way to draw a story from this stranger that related to the shooting on dock three. At this stage they forgot to 'act' immigration officers, because the task before them occupied all their resources. They had to think and behave like the people whose job they were engaged in; they had *become* immigration officers. The teacher who played the fugitive knew his cover story completely. Whether the children uncovered all or some of it depended on their skill in framing questions and listening constructively to his answers, given increasingly fluently but in broken English.

Stage Five
The teacher intervened at this stage, to bring together what had been discovered and to make the fugitive's situation clear. He was some kind of political refugee (the background was autocratic and he had a deposed and imprisoned father). He had killed a sailor who was trying to stop him leaving the ship on which he had stowed away. Should he be allowed sanctuary? The moral issues were complex: law, security, compassion, international relations, justice. The officers had to decide. Only when they had made a decision could the training officer voice an opinion. Then someone had to undertake to tell the fugitive his fate. He was escorted to the door by the teacher. She turned and announced the end of the play.

Conclusion
Each time this lesson was repeated with a different class, they made a unique decision based upon a series of options which they themselves suggested. These were: limited freedom, imprisonment, trial, temporary confinement while negotiating with the new regime in the fugitive's country, complete freedom, return, removal to another country, entry to this country for a trial period but only as a registered alien, and attempts to bring his family out. These were noted by the class teacher as potential areas for further lessons. The majority settled for trial in a court of law, with the chance of liberty if found not guilty of murder. They then had to find a way to explain this concept of justice to their anxious victim.

Further work
A lesson planned to include real objects and a fictional situation with theatrical devices and problem solving in role is not only the province of someone who works in the theatre. There are many teachers and students on teaching practice who would enjoy participating in a piece of pre-planned drama such as this. The level of acting required can be suited to the taste of the participants. The structure does not always have to be as rigid as this one, which had to be timed to last $1\frac{1}{2}$ hours. The central character can be adapted to suit a number of different circumstances: a woman appearing before a board of guardians during the Depression, a

tenant farmer in the potato famine, an immigrant, a dismissed worker before an appeal tribunal, a spaceman, someone suffering from loss of memory, a witch who has lost her powers, a case for rehousing. The list is endless. The only requirements are: a carefully prepared dossier for the role, someone to play the role who is prepared to reveal only a very little and then under pressure, and a good deal of preparatory role work by the class.

Even more may be gained from the idea of providing the class with a far less clearly defined situation: one which they may develop in a wider context than in the lesson quoted above, which had a highly structured dossier with significant props, and a set of pre-determined circumstances—the death of a foreign sailor. In a less highly structured set-up the class may be more inventive about the role figure and may actually feed information to the character, rather than extracting it as in *The fugitive*.

Lesson 5: Teaching the teacher—3rd year secondary boys

Objectives and Planning This group of boys had never done drama, so there was a dual purpose to the lesson. Higher up the school, drama was offered as an optional subject, and the teacher wanted to encourage the boys to enjoy working in this way. She also wanted to make drama accessible to them as a way of extending their work on a text, in this case a novel. The idea of 'teaching the teacher' is that the class is led 'unawares' into taking part, without realizing that they are acting. This goes against the previously emphasized honesty of approach, but in this case the teacher felt that their self-esteem was too delicate, and that a straightforward approach would not succeed. Failure at this stage would erode their confidence even further. They were projecting a tough image and they seemed firmly rooted to a conventional approach to learning—with books, behind desks. She introduced the lesson by saying that they were going to work on a part of the book they were studying, but with a different approach which aimed to find out more about the characters.

Stage One
The class's ability in reading aloud varied. The teacher usually read a passage and the class discussed it. In this case, the reading concerned a case of stealing from a shopkeeper. After the passage had been read the teacher opened the discussion. She asked if there were ways in which keepers of small newsagents shops could protect themselves. The boys made suggestions. The teacher pretended stupidity: 'You mean, if this desk was the counter and I were the shopkeeper, I would keep the cigarettes here and the newspapers and magazines over here?' A few minutes were spent in organizing the teacher as a shopkeeper, which led

into the next foolish query: 'But that means that it is impossible for anyone to steal cigarettes. How could anyone manage?' After a bit of wrangling over the merits of various approaches, the boys were very easily manoeuvred into showing where they would stand and how the teacher/shopkeeper would be distracted, by getting sweets from the top shelf while they slipped cigarettes into pockets. No one was acting. They were simply demonstrating an approach.

Stage Two
Before the boys returned to their seats the teacher set up a new line of enquiry, 'What would happen if someone else came in and saw the theft? Where would he be?' A stand-in was needed. The layout of the scene became more elaborate, but attention was still focused more on the method of achieving a result, than on the characters or the acting. The rest of the class were engaged in directing the action as well as watching.

Stage Three
Before the boys returned to their places the teacher introduced the idea that if the man knew the boys, he might be involved in some more significant way than if he were a stranger. 'Suppose he were a teacher, how would he be likely to react? What would he say?' The class suggested that he would report the boys to the headmaster.

Stage Four
Setting up the next scene followed relatively easily. The headmaster's study was represented by the desk. The boy playing the part of the teacher reported the incident to the head, the head spoke to the boys, the parents were sent for, the shopkeeper was pacified. All the time the teacher and the rest of the class made suggestions, although the teacher confined herself to asking leading questions, or saying 'Why don't we look at what would happen if . . .' in order to keep the lesson going.

Stage Five: Discussion
No mention was made of the fact that the class had been led into doing drama. This was taken as a matter of course. It was a different way of answering questions; that was all.

Conclusion
Of all the objectives that were set for this lesson the technique of introducing drama painlessly had been the most important. The subject matter might have been approached just as effectively by writing, discussion or further reading. Having introduced the technique at a very primitive level the teacher could encourage the class to go on to a deeper level of investigation of a piece of text. By having concentrated on attitudes rather than characteristics in their chosen roles, the boys had acted

without embarrassment or caricature, allowing the teacher to withdraw from the scene at an early stage.

Future Work
In further lessons the teacher continued to build up the level of the boys' involvement in the action by concentrating on questioning. A scene would be set up in the same prosaic way, but the class would have the right to 'freeze' it at some point and question the characters about their motivation. This is similar to the Stanislavsky approach to acting. Questioning someone in role produces a wealth of background information about the character. This can afterwards be checked against the information in the book, if the scenes are taken from, or parallel, a book. Questioning should not be undertaken in order to catch out or belittle a fellow pupil; it is simply done to elicit information about the possible motivation and feelings of a character. After having 'frozen' the scene to allow for questioning it may be resumed at any point, or a further scene may be requested.

Lesson 6: Journey to Karaganda—4th year secondary girls

Objectives The exercise was aimed at intensifying character work with a class that had opted to take drama as an examination course. At this stage in the academic year they were rather at odds with each other and could be unruly. They seemed to have difficulty in structuring their own work. The lesson occupied a double period.

Planning
The teacher made a number of uncompleted travel documents which asked for name, age, home town or village, occupation, husband's name and occupation, and the names and ages of any dependents. She also wrote three foreign-sounding place names on the board and prepared some folded slips of paper, one marked with a cross. She planned to use a tightly structured lesson plan, which set time limits for each section, the timing and structure to be an integral part of the theme and atmosphere of the play itself. Before the girls came into the room she arranged the chairs in four groups in the corners of the room and switched off some of the lights to increase the unwelcoming look of a bare room. The documents and other writing materials were set out on a couple of desks. As the girls came in they put away their bags and sat on the chairs, regrouping themselves automatically to sit next to their friends. The noisiest members of the class formed one of the four groups.

Stage One
The teacher introduced the subject of the drama. She mentioned that one of the criteria for their examination was the ability to sustain a role.

She was going to ask them to invent a character for themselves, which they would have to sustain for the whole lesson. They were to be women who had been taken away from home in the middle of the night. They were to imagine a place where it was not unusual for soldiers to turn out whole families and to separate them, the men taken off somewhere else, the elderly and the very young herded away. The women had been allowed to put on some clothes and take a few belongings and a blanket or two before being loaded into unheated railway carriages where they had been for some hours. They had no idea where they were. She asked each group to take the name of a place from the list and handed three groups travel documents and pencils. She gave them five minutes to complete them. They were encouraged to think that they were probably not British, that they were under suspicion, poor and frightened. She then turned to the more dominant fourth group. She told them quietly that they were to be the guards and that their job was to question the women in order to find out something about them and their families. They were to look out for any inconsistencies, for any mistakes, for any potential dissidents either among the women themselves or their families. They were to stick closely to the information on the travel documents. The teacher said that she would be the senior officer but that she would only interfere in extreme cases. They could use the desks and writing materials, organizing themselves as they pleased. They would then have twenty five minutes for questioning. The teacher returned to the other groups. Some of the girls had chosen to be members of the same family, which was not what she had intended, but she let it go. She had a couple of minutes' discussion with each group.

Stage Two
The teacher introduced a surprise element. She wanted to eliminate any chance of over-enthusiasm in the interrogation so she called for everyone's attention and announced a secret draw. Each of the women would be given a slip of paper. The one with a cross on it would be a spy. This gave a degree of reality to the search, a real objective as well as a dramatic objective. The guards would have more incentive to find the culprit if they thought there was someone deliberately falsifying her cover story. The teacher had to cheat here because some girls had opted for characters who were related and could therefore vouch for each other, so she made sure she gave the marked paper to a suitable character. She collected them up again and began the play.

Stage Three
Assuming the role of chief guard she addressed the assembled women. She explained that they had been taken off the train for questioning, that they should be patient and not cause trouble, that they would soon be taken on to the labour camp at Karaganda. She said that they would be

here for only half an hour while their papers were checked. She ordered the guards to collect the papers and call the names of those they wished to question first.

Stage Four

The guards had organized several interrogation points, with desks and chairs set out. While the questioning was going on the teacher refused to allow the other prisoners to talk openly, although she remained deaf to some subversive whispering. She interfered as little as possible, only reminding the guards about the time and answering direct questions. She refused to answer questions from the prisoners.

Stage Five

After the prisoners had been questioned the guards kept some suspicious characters on one side. Since all their papers had been taken away some of the women had given confused answers. The guards had been quite ruthless. The teacher had acted as a control to ensure that there was no undue aggression and that any animosity was kept firmly within the drama. It was nearly time to stop. The play could well have continued until all dubious characters were re-examined and only one suspect remained. However, the teacher's objective for the lesson had been achieved so she asked the guards to confer for a moment and then name the character they regarded as the chief suspect. They whispered excitedly and the tension among the women prisoners, on hearing their names, was quite dramatic. The suspect was named and the teacher asked who had played that part. One girl put up her hand. 'Were you the spy?' 'No.' 'Who had the marked card?' 'I did.' Everyone laughed. They were themselves again and the play was over.

Conclusion

The device of drawing lots was not essential to the drama. It made no real sense, in that every girl was inventing a cover story, so they were all equally fictional. However it established a motive for completing the exercise and a stronger set of controls. The class had maintained roles throughout and had benefitted from an imposed structure.

Further work

There was enough inherent drama in this situation to allow it to develop over several more sessions. The girls were keen to go on and the teacher was anxious to encourage them to work cooperatively and without such a rigid structure. The labour camp idea, if it were extended, would bring guards and prisoners into a kind of interdependence. Karaganda is the name of the camp in Solzhenitzyn's *The Love-Girl and the Innocent* and this play could serve as a reference point. There was a good deal of potential in the background stories of each of the girls' characters and these could be explored by means of flashbacks structured by the girls themselves.

7

Theatre as an art form

Performance

Public performance has been discussed elsewhere in this book and it may be that both class and teacher decide that their need to communicate with a wider audience necessitates a public showing of their work. This can be both a stimulus to creative work and a morale booster to young people who perhaps need the kudos of success because their achievement in other fields may be low.

Whatever reasons there may be for public performance, it should ideally be a matter of choice and not an accepted ritual of school life. Too many teachers find themselves bound to produce the school play, year after year, until it ceases to be a creative or artistic stimulus. In doing this they find their own classroom work suffers and they exhaust both themselves and their pupils. Not many people understand why a teacher who enjoys teaching and creating drama, does not necessarily regard a public performance as the climax of the work. The whole process is entirely different and should not be confused with the use of drama as a learning method.

If, however, we leave the school play outside the scope of this book, there is, nevertheless, a large body of work which comes within the definition of drama in school and which does concern itself with theatrical form.

There is a large increase in the number of candidates entered for examination in Drama and Theatre Arts and there are many younger children who are also fascinated by the mystery of theatrical form. In order to avoid the interest in theatrical techniques conflicting with the aims of the teacher in taking a class through the 'as if' acting process, it may be sensible to make a continuous and clear distinction throughout all the work, explaining and discussing the various methods used. Then when the class needs to examine technique more fully—not just as part of their normal work but as an adjunct to a visit to the theatre for example, or as a prelude to a public performance—they can call it 'Theatre Arts'.

Theatre Arts for examination

Dramatic literature forms a large part of our cultural heritage and therefore is part of the syllabus in most schools. As already described, there are many ways in which scripted material may be used in classroom drama, as there are many ways in which drama methods may be used to examine literary material. In order to gain the most from a study of theatre arts, pupils need to find for themselves the most expressive and appropriate way of handling the ideas they wish to convey. Most examination courses follow a somewhat similar pattern, and are usually spread over two years. First the students need to accustom themselves to working together as a group. They will probably spend some time on improvisation exercises and small sections of script, working 'on their feet', with the teacher serving as either a director or coordinator of their ideas. The next stage is to begin to direct the work outwards, and at this level the most useful approach seems to be aimed at practising the various ways of conveying meaning.

As described earlier, the performer needs to find the most appropriate symbols to reveal to an audience his understanding of a character. Classroom performers will probably want to refine action, words, narrative and grouping until they can convey the required meaning to an audience. Pupils should be able to discipline their own creativity by rehearsing mime techniques, by observing character in words and movement, by selecting appropriate language, observing climaxes, shaping narrative and working on grouping and the creation of stage pictures. In order to further this disciplining process, teachers often encourage pupils to keep a notebook or diary to record progress and promote self-criticism.

Criticism can be very destructive. Because performers are using all of themselves—body and voice, head, heart and emotion—they can be easily hurt by even the most sympathetic personal criticism. Yet obviously criticism is absolutely vital if there is to be any objectivity in the work, any idea of achievement and if high standards are to be achieved. Criticism of this kind is best done by class and teacher together, not as a verdict at the end, but to find points for further development during work on the scene. The teacher can say, 'There's a bit that doesn't seem to work ... I mean the section where the girl comes back from the court-house with the news of the verdict. That ought to be a climax but it doesn't seem to register as very important. There are two ways we can do this. Either we change the girl's entrance so that she is the focus of everyone's attention and she speaks even louder and more emphatically, or we see the effect of what she says—quite softly and without any drama—by the way everyone reacts. Let's try it the first way and see if it improves, then we can look at the other and decide which looks best from out here.' In this way no one is singled out as having done wrong, and providing they have all tried to achieve something, nobody is blamed for the failure of the scene. Also the methods (placing, audibility, reaction, focus, concentration, belief) are all recognized and worked at so that another time they may be used in another, similar scene. If then the student writes up a diary, recording the work, he or she may be helped to become self-critical and therefore confident of improvement rather than resentful of others' opinions.

In the professional theatre there are some directors who give people private and individual help and criticism, others who give all their notes in public. In a school situation, attention to the work in hand is probably best done before the whole group, without any 'secret' individual attention.

At some stage in the first year of an examination course there is usually a set objective. The work is shown to outsiders, maybe an examiner or moderator, as well as to the rest of the year, or to a group of other children from a neighbouring primary or special school. Some objective for the work both limits and concentrates the range, as well as providing a sense of occasion. The scale of performance does not need to be very large. A programme of puppet plays, a documentary programme, scenes (improvised or scripted) on a theme, even an unprepared piece of drama work of the kind normally undertaken by the class, becomes a performance when the moderator comes into the school, and the need for communication skills becomes immediately apparent before a stranger.

Some courses require more written work than others but most have a section where the student submits a project. It always seems a great shame that so many projects remain so uncreative. Projects are sometimes chosen because there are reference books in the library, not because the pupil has something personal to offer. Some of the most memorable project work has involved the same sympathetic and understanding creativity as the best drama work. Examples include: a scheme of music and movement exercises to be undertaken by young, blind children in a residential home; an educational theatre programme about Red Indians for a primary school; a shadow-puppet theatre; a model setting for a television play; a home-made radio play; make-up, with slides of work done; a study of a local theatre; a tape of guitar music improvised around a study of *Macbeth*; a mask and costume for a mime play. Projects can always be allied with a viva if there is felt to be some difficulty about assessing them. Usually an exhibition of the drama department's project work is a source of great pride to everyone.

A theatre arts course usually involves a certain number of theatre visits and a study of style and production methods. Usually the group are asked to undertake a more advanced piece of theatre work themselves, often a full-scale, scripted play or a rehearsed and presented piece of improvisation, which may be performed to an audience or to the examiner, usually in the fifth (the final) term of the course. Because of the difficulty of finding good, suitable material many schools devise their own, working up a programme which follows a thematic approach. The best way to tackle this seems to be to stockpile vast amounts of material—poems, magazine articles and pictures, selections of scenes from plays, pupils' own scripts and recorded improvisations—and then to experiment, by trying them out in rough performance, to see which piece successfully conveys the theme, as well as which piece allows the pupil sufficient scope to obtain an appropriate grade in the examination.

Performance as an art

Even without the goal of examinations, public performance can be a creative and productive end to a course in theatre arts. The opportunity, well known to the professional actor, of behaving in disguise as he would never behave in real life and being applauded for it, is a powerful feeling. Behaving in an uncharacteristic fashion and being able to control that behaviour and refine its expression, can be creative and exciting. In this case the methods used to convey the creativity to others become very important both to the performer and to the audience. In this country we take the training of young musicians and young dancers more seriously and more sensitively than the training of young actors. There is no reason why the talented youngster should not be encouraged. A more informed attitude about the state of the theatrical profession might prevent the head-in-air attitude of so many young people who think that success in the theatre is a matter of luck, rather than talent, practice and training. The example of music is a good one to apply, where many L.E.A.s take musical training as a natural part of the cultivation of individual skill in young children without thinking that it might encourage entry into an overcrowded profession. Also because of primitive feelings that good acting is the same as successful deceit, many people still regard the actor as different from 'normal' people and are suspicious.

Good performance skills can be related to the other arts and encouraged like any other gift. Children can be helped to realize ideas, as a member of a group working on 'communication through art'. To do this successfully standards must be high. Cooperation between teachers who have different skills can be seen by the pupils to be part of a group effort. Performance can, and should, call for skill in design, choreography, music, make-up, costume and lighting, and should be undertaken as a group activity which puts teachers and pupils on an equal footing.

School performances need not follow the usual progress from playreading, through blocking-in the moves, to dress rehearsal. A typical scheme of work might be that followed by a group of twelve-year-olds, who undertook to do Ben Jonson's *Every Man in His Humour*.

The children lived in the East End of London near the City and Hoxton where the play is set. This gave the choice of play some point. No one bothered to tell them that Jonson lived some 300 years ago or that his plays were considered difficult.

They were told that the play was mostly about a young man who wanted to get off on his own and have a good time. The idea of characters 'whose names tell you what they are like' was introduced and a good deal of discussion followed. The director took large sheets of lining paper and with large felt-tip pens drew, to the children's dictation, a type-figure for each name. Since they were type-figures there was no set period to the characters' looks, they simply carried a recognizable set of images. To clarify the images, a passage or two of Jonson's profuse words were read over so that, for example, Bobadil was not just any braggart soldier but a master of different kinds of weapons.

On subsequent meetings of the group the casting was done. Without knowing which was the 'best' part they mostly chose their own roles, or suggested who could best portray each character. Then the director told them a small section of the plot for each set of characters. Sometimes everyone would work on one piece, sometimes they would divide and work by themselves in smaller groups. After each scene had been refined and character, action and attitudes had been established using their own words, the director would suggest that the following week they could repeat that scene with the script. From Ben Jonson's play, the most appropriate lines would be typed up and given to the actors in that scene. If more were needed they could be found. If absolutely necessary they could be re-written. (Jonson is not subject to copyright and anyway he wrote more than these young actors needed so rewriting was not often necessary.) Thus the final script emerged, not by cutting an original to size, but by building towards the final version.

Everyone cooperated on the continuity of the narrative, on the provision of necessary 'props' and on costumes that tallied with the original drawings. Half-masks were used to suggest the images in the drawings and the scenery was painted by the actors themselves, based on a 16th century picture map of the area.

The final performance was not as long as the original play but it was a piece of work in which the spirit of the original was faithfully maintained and in which every young performer had determined his or her own contribution from beginning to end. Nobody had been drilled into fulfilling a director's fancy, nobody had been pushed out of his or her depth. Everyone had been extended in the range of his or her performance yet had remained in control of his or her own contribution.

This system is probably the way most companies worked in the early years of professional theatre, when they had a playwright as one of the company. It is a very satisfactory way for most youth theatre groups to operate, although it works best when the playwright is alive and present to record the improvisations and to provide the final script. Many teachers will find, however, that this child-centered approach to creating a performance is extremely useful. It can be applied to traditional material such as the Nativity, or to various ballads and legends just as well as to full-length classics. It ensures that the participants fully appreciate and understand what it is they are conveying and allows them to remain totally in command and confident in performance.

Conclusion

During the last few years the climate of opinion has changed radically with regard to educational drama. Teaching techniques have varied widely as people achieved success in directing young peoples' theatre, improvised plays, or music and movement. Developments in educational theatre have led to the establishment of much valuable work by professional T.I.E. companies. Nowadays teachers in general are looking to simulation, role-play and classroom drama as methods of enriching their own teaching. There seems, however, a danger of over-specialization. Just recently the idea of using drama as a method of teaching, rather than as an experience in its own right, has caused some teachers to devalue the characteristics of drama itself. If a group of young people have worked together creatively, have listened to other people's ideas and absorbed them into an artistic whole, have put on the mantle of another personality and observed with sensitivity the feel of another place or another time, isn't that enough? Must the teachers always set the factual or academic content above the human and emotional experience?

Drama can and should be a way in which important issues are explored. It can be a way of experiencing for oneself unattainable and extraordinary circumstances. It can be used in the teaching of literature, history, religious knowledge, politics, social studies and geography, to name but a few. However, the making of a satisfactory play, the creation of fiction, the belief in a symbolic action, such as driving back the flood waters to build a new city, have a value of their own, apart from the subject matter.

Looking back to the classic model of a drama teacher, the aim which seems paramount is developing the ability to *use* one's imagination. Maybe it is not possible to *develop* imagination but it is very possible to *use* it. The drama teacher by encouraging the willing suspension of disbelief is allowing children to use their imagination in a constructive and understanding way. Participation in such a creative exercise can be both enjoyable and exciting and can provide another way of achieving understanding. It is certainly high time that we got rid of the idea that drama is a noisy, chaotic activity that takes children away from their normal lessons. However much one emphasizes that drama is a different activity from book-learning, it is not outside the scope of the average lesson. No teacher should feel unduly threatened by embarking on classroom drama. Those teachers who have been encouraged to think of drama as something that can be undertaken in the same room as reading and writing, have been heartened by the ease with which the class have taken on some exercise in simple role-play, or taken the chance to get on their feet and work out a problem for themselves.

All our drama work should have the greatest possible attention paid to its content, to its appropriateness to the well-being of the young people concerned, and to both its imaginative and its emotional qualities. Making an artistic experience of a piece of life is a most satisfying and necessary part of growing. As teachers we can be enriched by making drama accessible to ourselves and to our pupils.

Appendix: Resources

Theatres

Many local authorities have an interest, financial or otherwise, in a professional theatre company. There may be a T.I.E. (Theatre in Education) company in the area whose job is to use theatrical methods to illuminate certain educational areas. Most of these companies welcome contact with teachers. Discussion on the nature and content of the programmes, follow-up work and feedback from the pupils are all fruitful and necessary parts of the association between T.I.E. companies and the schools.

Commercial theatres sometimes run their own T.I.E. companies or they may do special performances or workshops on set texts. Some theatres employ specially trained actor/teachers, others have a liaison officer whose responsibility is specifically educational, others merely maintain an interest in encouraging a young audience to come into the theatre.

Because theatre working hours are long and demanding, most theatres do not have the resources or time available to handle individual queries on 'how a theatre works'. Nonetheless, backstage tours can sometimes be arranged and every theatre welcomes a well planned and well prepared visit from an audience of young people who understand and appreciate a live theatre performance. Sometimes children do not understand that actors can see and hear the audience. They think that theatre is the same as film or television where one can walk about and talk without disturbing the performance. Children need to be trained to go to the theatre, even to understand and appreciate a performance in school, and it is essential to prepare them beforehand.

Actors may be persuaded to visit a school individually to work with a teacher and a class, but this is usually done on a personal basis and most actors are nervous of such contact and feel the need for some kind of structure to the visit.

Drama advisors

Advice is obtainable almost everywhere in the country either from a County Drama Advisor or from advisory teachers. There are often courses ranging from those of a brief in-service nature to longer courses offering qualifications varying from diplomas to B.Ed. There is a good deal to be gained from making contact with other teachers, even if it is only to share problems. Often the knowledge that a school will lend an essential spotlight or that the girls' school would love to do a joint production with the boys' can be both a comfort and a solution to a problem. The reassurance gained from meeting other teachers can be enormous and ideas can be easily pooled and talked over at informal meetings. Many advisors run summer schools where young people can engage in more advanced theatre techniques and some L.E.A.s run youth theatre groups. The position with regard to grants for further study and opportunities for attending larger, national or international youth theatre organizations varies from area to area but is worth investigating.

Television, film and radio

Local resources are often readily available, visits to studios are sometimes possible and the use of broadcast or other media material is often underrated as a stimulus. Many schools make their own programmes and this is an excellent way of getting to look at one's own work, or of working towards an end product. Published material is not only available under an educational heading, but many television and radio scripts are published and obtainable from libraries and bookshops, as well as from the broadcasting companies themselves.

Equipment

Many drama departments in schools find themselves in temporary need of equipment for stage effects, music reproduction, lighting and so on. Sometimes this can be borrowed. Most of it can be hired. Many theatres and studios have to throw away scenery because they cannot afford storage space. Usually if transport can be arranged, scenery can be obtained cheaply or even free. Exhibitions also throw out display material, which, when added to the blocks or rostra, curtains, and dressing-up box that are available in most schools, can flesh out a full-scale production in the hall. The person to contact at the theatre or studio is the production manager.

Other equipment such as tape-recorders, cameras, musical instruments, make-up and so on, are likely to be part of the normal stock. It does not always have to be of professional quality; for example, sound effects and make-up can be acquired from things readily available at home, and jumble sales provide the basis for many excellent wardrobes. Further details on the use of significant props may be found in the section on visual aids in *Beginning the lesson*.

Classroom drama requires very little, if any, elaborate equipment. The greatest luxury is a sufficient amount of time in a quiet place, enough chairs and writing materials available to hand.

Texts

Play texts suffer from being marked and carried about during rehearsals. It is usually better to have scripts for performance as single copies, one for each actor. Collections of plays intended for class work are too expensive to be subjected to wear and tear during rehearsals. Nevertheless they may be needed for reading and work in the classroom. Sometimes sets can be hired or borrowed from local authority educational libraries or from commercial agencies.

Information

Sources of information vary from one area to another. Often the drama advisor can help to track down equipment or copies of useful scripts. The following addresses may be helpful. The periodicals carry advertisements and addresses of suppliers to both professional and amateur companies, as well as to schools.

Drama, British Theatre Association, 9 Fitzroy Square, London W1P 6AE. (sets of play scripts for hire)
British Theatre Directory, John Offord (Publications) Ltd., PO Box 64, Eastbourne, East Sussex, BN21 3LW. (useful addresses)
Speech & Drama, Society of Teachers of Speech and Drama, 7 Rowan Avenue, Northampton.
Creative Drama, Educational Drama Association, Reaside School, Reaside Street, Birmingham 5.
Insight/Outlook, NADECT (National Association for Drama in Education & Children's Theatre), 50 Lindrosa Road, Streetly, Sutton Coldfield, West Midlands.
London Drama, Drama & Tape Centre, Princeton Street, London WC1.
National Association for the Teaching of Drama, 20 Tamworth Park, Mitcham, Surrey.
Community Service Volunteers, 237 Pentonville Road, London, N1 (simulation games and other material)
2D, (Drama/Dance) Advisory Centre, Education Department, County Hall, Glenfield, Leicester LE3 8RF.

Bibliography

Works mentioned in the text

Kipling, Rudyard, *Puck of Pooks Hill*, Macmillan.

Nesbit, E., *Five Children and It*, Puffin Books.

Stanislavsky, Constantin (translated by E. R. Hapgood), *An Actor prepares*, Geoffrey Bles.

Stanislavsky, Constantin (translated by E. R. Hapgood), *Building a Character*, Reinhardt & Evans.

White, T. H., *The Once and Future King*, Collins.

Bond, Edward, *Saved*, Methuen.

Solzhenitsyn, Alexander, *The Love-Girl and the Innocent*, Penguin Books.

Sophocles, *Œdipus Rex*, Penguin Books

Books for Further Reading

Allen, John, *Drama in Schools: Its Theory and Practice*, Heinemann Educational.

Bolton, Gavin, *Towards a Theory of Drama in Education*, Longman.

Brooke, Peter, *The Empty Space*, Penguin Books.

Courtney, Richard, *Play, Drama and Thought*, Cassell.

Day, Christopher, *Drama for Middle and Upper Schools*, Batsford.

Fines and Verrier, *The Drama of History*, New University Education.

Leach, Robert, *How to Make a Documentary Play*, Blackie.

O'Neill, Cecily and Lambert, Alan, *Drama Structures*, Hutchinson.

O'Neill, Lambert, Linnell, Warr-Wood, *Drama Guidelines*, Heinemann Educational.

Self, David, *A Practical Guide to Drama in Secondary Schools*, Ward Lock Educational.

Wagner, Betty Jane, *Dorothy Heathcote: Drama as a Learning Medium*, Hutchinson.